This book will help you

Smarten the F*ck Up!

...or at least sound like it!

By: Dave Bastien

Dedication

I can't tell you how many times I've browsed through comments on social media posts and said, "I wish people would smarten the f*ck up!" Then one day I decided to do something about it.

This book is dedicated to all those whose comments were so bad that I finally said, "These people need some help... I've got to write this f*cking book!" It never would have happened without you.

Contents

Author's Note

Yes, I was inspired to write this book out of frustration from reading mistakes in social media comments. But I have to admit – I make mistakes, too (although, like many people, I blame most of them on auto-correct). ;-)

I'm admitting to my own mistakes because I want to make it clear that, although I have a strong foundation, I'm not a grammar expert. I'm just very curious about the English language. I look things up... *a lot*. I look up words, metaphors, grammar, origins of sayings, etc., and if someone says something I don't understand, I grab my portable encyclopedic device (my phone) and research it. Occasionally, I learn something, but more often I find they've made a mistake.

All my research went into a file of common mistakes that I compiled over several years, and that's where this book came from. The title, *Smarten the F*ck Up*, came to me long before I started writing, and I've tried to ensure the content reflects that attitude. I think a book that's largely about grammar – typically a boring subject – needs to be spiced up to make it more engaging to help people learn. So what you'll find within these pages is some humor, a bit of sarcasm, a touch of crudeness, a dose of politics, a little cursing here and there, a few random expressions of humanity, as well as a tongue-in-cheek irreverence toward grammar nerds. You'll also see an occasional rant, but just for the sake of entertainment. It's definitely not your typical grammar book!

But I really want to help people learn, too, because I truly believe that when people can communicate more effectively they can increase their opportunities in life – economically and otherwise.

I've learned a lot from writing this book, and I sincerely I hope it finds its way into the hands of those who need it.

I look at it this way...

People appreciate when a friend tells them they have toilet paper stuck to their shoe. They also appreciate being told when they have food stuck in their teeth. Having a friend who saves you from embarrassment is usually welcomed, but unfortunately, most of us don't have a friend who points out the embarrassing things we say. *This book is that friend!*

Acknowledgements

First, I need to acknowledge my wife, Sue (or Susan, as she calls herself – it took her 10 years to correct me so I can't change now). As I compiled my notes of common mistakes, she patiently indulged my annoying habit of listening for and correcting common mistakes by people on TV and radio (and sometimes her, too, but only for research purposes, of course). She's actually developed the same habit and has become pretty good at it. I know it can be very annoying, though, so I'm hoping the habit will fade now that this book is done. We'll see how it goes, but in the meantime, she's been a trooper and incredibly supportive.

My second acknowledgement goes to my sister, Donna, who probably taught me as much about grammar as the Catholic school nuns who whacked my knuckles with a wooden ruler whenever I got it wrong. Having someone to call with stupid grammar questions is like having unlimited access to your favorite English teacher. Her patience is amazing! She's a professional editor of books and journal articles now, while also translating them from French to English (in her second career, because she thinks it's fun – *imagine that!*), and she graciously offered to help edit this book.

Dave Bastien

Preface

So why would you want to *Smarten the F*ck Up*, anyway?

Social media platforms have exposed just how uneducated much of our society is today (and I'm only referring to grammar, of course).

I often cringe as I read comments from friends, including many "friends" I don't really know, as is the case for most of us on social media. I struggle against the urge to correct their mistakes, and try to stay focused on the content, but it's hard sometimes.

I know others have also had this experience. There are times when I'm out having a few beers with friends and one of them will check their social media accounts and point out someone's blatant grammar mistake. Then a discussion ensues where we all recognize friends who are chronic abusers. (I'm sure several of your friends' names are popping into your head as you read this. Now you can just drop a link to this book on their comments.) ;-)

The point is, everyone seems to remember who-said-what that made them sound stupid, and they can usually cite examples, too. *The fact that others remember someone's habitual mistakes says a lot about the impression poor grammar has on people.* You don't want to be that someone!

Many of the common mistakes covered in this book go beyond grammar. And whether it's our grammar, misused words or phrases, or incorrect punctuation, how we communicate affects how people perceive our intelligence and professionalism. In many cases we don't even realize we're making mistakes… *but others do!*

You're probably not even aware, in the moment, that someone is making a snap judgment about you because of your grammar. It may not be fair, but it happens. It may also be what puts you at the top – or the bottom – of the candidate pool when you interview for your dream job.

And if the potential of not getting your dream job isn't enough motivation for you to *Smarten the F*ck Up*, maybe this will be: dumb mistakes can ruin your chances with your online dating profile, too!

And that's why you want to *Smarten the F*ck Up*.

Introduction

Yes, talking about grammar is boring. And reading books and websites about grammar is confusing as hell and can make your head explode. Most people who really want to improve their grammar would never make it through a single sentence of an explanation written by a grammar nerd. For instance, how far would you get if a page started with a sentence like this?

An object pronoun is a type of personal pronoun that is normally used as a grammatical object, either as the direct or indirect object of a verb, or as the object of a preposition.

Most people would think, "Huh? WTF!" If you're like me, you probably couldn't even finish reading that sentence. You won't find any of that here! I avoid grammar-technical rules and other word-nerd terms because with that kind of language, you'd stop reading immediately and learn nothing. That's master-level stuff, and I'm more of a jack-of-all-trades kinda guy.

It's elementary

A lot of this book's content may seem elementary – that's because it is. I learned grammar in a Franco-American Catholic grammar school (also called *elementary* school) where the nuns drilled it into your head – figuratively – so that's the level you'll find here. It's *elementary*, which, unfortunately, still seems to be elusive to many. I hope this book helps fix that.

I deciphered the experts, so you don't have to!

My research for this book took me to books and websites written by experts, and I soon realized that their explanations were written as if intended for other grammar experts. What good is that?! I've done my best to translate their grammar-speak into language the average non grammar nerd – like me – can understand. *This book ain't for experts!*

Here's a general rule I discovered:

It takes 99% of your effort to understand the 1%, but only 1% of your effort to understand the 99%.

The 1% represents the exceptions to just about every grammar rule that, in general, are ways of speaking that the average person would never use, or at least not very often. I don't worry about being wrong 1% of the time. *I'll take that.* My goal is to make you sound smarter 99% of the time, which I'm sure will be an improvement if you're reading this book! ;-)

Focus on the 99%

If you look up any grammar rule, you'll find that with just a bit of determination you can understand 99% of it, especially through the examples. It's the 1% that ties your brain into a f*cking knot. Yet all grammar books and websites lead with grammar-nerd rules and descriptions that make you shut down immediately, when you could have at least become 99% smarter!

That 99% is the focus of this book! With it, you'll be able to fix most of the basic mistakes we all make from time to time and you'll sound 99% smarter with 1% of the effort.

Disclaimer: Please keep this in mind as you read this book

I don't live nearly as interesting a life as some of the example sentences in this book may lead you to believe. They're constructed solely to provide a bit of entertainment and humor on a topic that's typically pretty boring. They're born from my imagination (in most cases) and in no way represent my own actions, activities, or values, even though some people may dispute this disclaimer. ;-)

Also, while parts of this book might seem a bit condescending, I'm really not trying to talk down to anyone. I'm just trying to make sure my points are understood and not assuming everyone will understand something that may seem simple to others.

For instance, since my early days of writing I've followed the advice of Robert Louis Stevenson: "Don't write merely to be understood. Write so that you cannot possibly be misunderstood." I believe this is especially important when writing about grammar, so that's been my goal in this book. To accomplish this goal with grammar requires a bit more effort and maybe some over-simplification, so I hope you don't find it condescending, but rather helpful.

There are a few instances where I've had to walk on the edge of being a grammar nerd. Those occur only where it's important to the lesson and there's no other way to simplify the topic. In those cases, I've tried to provide elementary examples to make the explanations as simple as dirt. If those sections screw you into the ceiling, just skip 'em. There's lots more to learn!

In summary, I have three goals with this book:

1. Make you 99% smarter.

My most important goal is to focus on the 99%. As I've said, it's typically the 1% exceptions that make your head spin to the point where you want to throw the book into the fire – unless you're reading it on your iPad, of course. (I stay away from the 1% because iPads are expensive.)

2. Refrain from using grammar-nerd language as much as possible.

Grammar-nerd speak just makes people feel frustrated and dumb, so I avoid it as much as *humanely* possible. ;-)

3. Make it fun and entertaining for you to *Smarten the F*ck Up!*

I truly believe that people learn better when they're engaged and that humor creates engagement. Interesting examples make rules easier to remember, especially when you can relate to them through humor, so I hope you enjoy my sometimes-odd sense of humor.

Guarantee

I guarantee that following the advice in this book will make you sound 99% smarter, but you might lose a few friends along the way. Once you start learning to correct *your* grammar, it's a short slide to correcting your family's and friends' grammar too, so be careful. If you find that happening, put the book down for a while – or just buy them a copy and you can *Smarten the F*ck Up* together!

Regarding the guarantee… if you don't feel smarter after reading this book, send me a note and I'll refund your money. I can't be held responsible for what happens with your friends when you begin correcting them, though.

Believe me when I say I'm no expert, but I've pretty much got the basics down... *and I believe you can too,* so read on, and let's get started!

Instructions

Yes, this grammar book comes with a few simple instructions. Here are three ways you can get the most out of this book:

1. Don't read it straight through

Don't go through it like a regular book. There are chapters you'll get stuck on, and that's okay. Skip them before your brain starts to pulse and is on the verge of hemorrhaging. There's plenty more to learn, so skip what you need to and read on.

2. Use the table of contents

Use it to jump to chapters of interest to you. Those that catch your attention are likely the ones you'll learn the most from.

3. Share it with a friend

Share it with a friend, your significant other, or a family member. Ask them what chapters jump out at them. When you discuss these topics with someone else, you learn more yourself because everyone sees things through a slightly different lens and discussion brings clarity.

That's it! I hope you have a wonderful, fun, and entertaining learning experience. It's time to *Smarten the F*ck Up!*

Dave Bastien

I vs. Me

You may think *I* vs. *me* is an easy thing to master, but it's one that way too many people f*ck up every day. If you're one of the habitual misusers of *I* vs. *me,* here's a simple rule to always get it right:

The rule: Take the other person out of the sentence and say it again.

Example 1 – wrong: "My brother got hit in the nuts while playing catch with my sister and *I.*"

Simply take *my sister* out (not really… she's married now, so you can't). Now it reads: "My brother got hit in the nuts while playing catch with *I.*"

This obviously sounds wrong, right? (If it sounds right to you, then just put this book down immediately and walk away... or give it to a friend, because it's not going to help you.)

The correct way to say it, when *my sister* is out of the sentence, is: "My brother got hit in the nuts while playing catch with *me.*"

So, putting the full sentence back together, we get:

Example 1 – correct: "My brother got hit in the nuts while playing catch with my sister and *me.*"

And if you're worried about my brother, don't. He's got kids now, so he's fine.

Here's another example of the kind of thing I hear often:

Example 2 – wrong: "When you're done organizing the Super Bowl party can you let Brenda and *I* know what the cost is?"

Now, I'm certainly not going to correct someone's grammar if they're paying for the party! And this might sound perfectly fine to you, but it's not. Here's why:

Take *Brenda* out of the sentence (she didn't want to be sentenced to attending this work-related party anyway), and you're left with:

"When you're done organizing the Super Bowl party can you let *I* know what the cost is?" Again, it's obviously not correct! Following the *I* vs. *me* rule, the sentence should be:

> **Example 2 – correct:** "When you're done organizing the Super Bowl party can you let Brenda and *me* know what the cost is?"

There are many times when *I* should be *me*. And I'm not talking about a life lesson on being your authentic self; I mean it literally: this rule will always help you know when the word *I* should be changed to *me*.

Just a formality? No!

Some people confuse *I* and *me* because they mistakenly think *I* is more formal than *me*. Using the wrong word because you think it sounds more formal is called *hypercorrection*. A common example is when someone says, "between you and *I*," when they should say "between you and *me*." So I'll just say that, between you and me, it's much better to be correct than (mistakenly) formal.

It really is that simple. Got it? Good! Now let's move on.

Me vs. Myself

More than 90% of the people I know make this mistake!

By far, the most common misuse of *me* vs. *myself* is people saying *myself* when they should be saying *me*. And here's the easy part of using *me* vs. *myself*: the rule is the same as in the previous chapter!

<u>The rule</u>: Take the other person out of the sentence and say it again.

> **Example 1 – wrong:** "Maggie was very proud of her new implants and sent pictures of them to Jimmy and *myself*."

To find the correct word, simply take *Jimmy* out of the group (even though he'd be disappointed to not get the pics) and re-write the sentence: "Maggie was very proud of her new implants and sent pictures of them to *myself*." This obviously doesn't sound right, so the correct word to use is *me*, as in "Maggie was very proud of her new implants and sent pictures of them to *me*."

Then you can add Jimmy back in and get the correct version of the full sentence, which is:

> **Example 1 – correct:** "Maggie was very proud of her new implants and sent pictures of them to Jimmy and *me*." (I still don't know why she included Jimmy in this, though.)

Here's a simple rule on when to use *myself*: If you use the word *I* at or near the beginning of the sentence, you should typically use *myself*. Otherwise, use *me*.

I call it the "*I, Myself*" rule because that's the order of the words as they appear in a sentence when *myself* is used correctly. This is the 99% rule and covers almost all instances of when you'd use the word *myself*. And it certainly covers enough to make you sound 99% smarter, which, after all, is the goal of this book!

For example, if I'm the one sending the pictures of Maggie's new implants to myself, then I'd use *I* at the beginning of the sentence and it would be like this:

"*I* sent the pictures of Maggie's new implants to *myself.*"

And if I also sent them to Jimmy then it would read, "*I* sent the pictures of Maggie's new implants to Jimmy and *myself.*" And he would thank me. After all – as he finally explained to me – he's the one who recommended the dentist she got them from!

Here's another common example of misusing *myself*:

> **Example 2 – wrong:** "The farting contest at the bar last night was started by Jimmy and *myself.*" Again, taking Jimmy out, it's wrong to say, "The farting contest at the bar last night was started by *myself.*"

Here's the correct version:

> **Example 2 – correct:** "The farting contest at the bar last night was started by Jimmy and *me.*" It's also correct to say, if you take Jimmy out, "The farting contest at the bar last night was started by *me.*" (But if you take Jimmy out then it's not really a contest… unless you can find another willing participant.)

Important: These examples show that if the word *I* doesn't appear before the word *myself,* chances are 99.99% that you should use the word *me.*

P.S. A friend of mine who read this chapter said that anyone who sharts in a farting contest automatically wins. I told him that was disgusting and gross. He said, "Let's have a contest!"

I thought I was a competitive bastard, but I would never go that far to win a contest. I say, "Uncle!"

She, He & I
vs.
Her, Him & Me

I know, I know... the title of this chapter is so engaging that it's the first one you want to read... not! But as you read through it, I think you'll find this mistake, which is all too common, is an easy one to fix. And you may be a bit embarrassed that you got it wrong for so many years. Let's get into the details...

Sometimes we don't do things alone. Sometimes *she* and *I* do things together. And sometimes Jimmy comes over to watch a game with *her* and *me*. Sometimes *he* and *I* go to Billy's Sports Bar to watch the game. And sometimes *she* comes to the sports bar with *him* and *me*. It's nice to have people to do things with. And it's nice to be able to post it correctly on social media to let all your other friends know what they're missing out on!

***She*, *he* & *I* and *her*, *him* & *me* are all pronouns.** Pronouns are simply words that take the place of nouns, as in this case, where they take the place of the names of the people involved.

This is another area where people are easily confused, but again, there's a simple rule to get it right, and – how easy is this – it's the same rule as the previous two chapters!

<u>The rule</u>: Take the other person(s) out of the sentence and say it again.

Here's a simple example:

> **Example 1 – wrong**: "*Her* and *I* had a few beers at the game."
> Also wrong: "*Him* and *I* had a few beers at the game."

If you take the *I* out of the first sentence, it reads: "*Her* had a few beers at the game." This is obviously wrong! It sounds fine if you say, "*She* had a few beers at the game." But you never want anyone to drink alone, so the correct version is:

Example 1 – correct: "*She* and *I* had a few beers at the game." Also correct: "*He* and *I* had a few beers at the game."

This is a very common mistake. If I corrected everyone I've heard make it, I'd risk losing all my friends. So I'm careful about who I correct. ;-)

It's also an example of a mistake people make because they think it sounds smarter. It doesn't. Here's another example:

Example 2 – wrong: "Rick came over and found *she* and *I* sleeping in the hammock."

To confirm it's wrong simply remove one of the people involved and say it again: "Rick came over and found *she* sleeping in the hammock." Or "Rick came over and found *I* sleeping in the hammock." Both are clearly mistakes.

Let's fix it one person at a time to confirm the correct way to say it: "Rick came over and found *her* sleeping in the hammock." Or, "Rick came over and found *me* sleeping in the hammock." There you go! They both sound fine. Now you know the correct way to say the full sentence, which is:

Example 2 – correct: "Rick came over and found *her* and *me* sleeping in the hammock." Isn't that simple?

The grammar-nerd rule (with examples below):

- *She, he,* and *I* are **subject pronouns**. These should be used when referring to the subject of the sentence, meaning who the sentence is about or who is doing the action.
- *Her, him,* and *me* are **object pronouns**. These should be used when referring to the object of the sentence, meaning the one(s) receiving the action.

To recap, they're all *pronouns*, taking the place of a noun – a person, place, or thing. In this case they're *personal pronouns*, because they take the place of the person's name. This subject/object relationship holds true in each of the correct examples above.

If this explanation just muddled your mind, go get a beer and come back to read the simple-as-dirt examples below... I'll wait!

Are you back? Okay, here are some simple examples:

> **Example 1:** "*She* hates *him*." *She* is the subject (doing the hating), and the object of her hate is *him*.

> **Example 2:** "*He* loves *her*." In this case *he* is the subject (doing the loving), and the object of his love is *her*. (Even though *she* hates *him* in the first example... but isn't that all too common in relationships?)

> **Example 3:** "*She* and *I* threw jello at *him*." *She* and *I* together are the subject (a compound subject, meaning more than one) and the object of our jello throwing is *him*. (It was her idea!)

> **Example 4:** "*He* made fun of *me* for not knowing the difference between a subject and an object in a sentence." *He* is the subject, and the object of his humiliation is *me*.

Once you understand the subject/object sentence structure, you can avoid making mistakes in using these two groups of personal pronouns. If this is too grammar-nerdy for you, don't worry. There's plenty more to learn that's simple as pi. (That's a math joke, because I'm writing this chapter on 3/14. It's okay if you don't get it. It's just a nerdy joke.)

On to the next big mistake!

Fewer vs. Less

This one is pretty simple, too, although even when you know the rule it takes a while to catch yourself before the words jump out of your mouth.

The 99% rule: When referring to something you can count, use *fewer*, otherwise, use *less*. Think *individual things* vs. *a bunch of stuff.*

- *Fewer* means not as many *things* that can be counted.
- *Less* means not as much *stuff* you can't count.

It doesn't take a brain surgeon to tell the difference, but if I ever needed a brain surgeon I don't think I'd worry about their grammar.

Here are some examples of using *less* vs. *fewer*:

Example 1 – wrong: "He decided to buy Bud Light because it had *less* calories than Heineken."

Example 1 – correct: "He decided to buy Bud Light because it had *fewer* calories than Heineken, but even though the calories could be counted, it was obvious he never did."

(He's probably a cheap SOB too, because Bud Light tastes like skunk piss, and for just 31 fewer calories it would be difficult to drink even if you were dying of thirst in Death Valley.)

Here's another example:

Example 2 – wrong: "Ma, you gave me *less* meatballs than Timmy!"

Meatballs are pretty easy to count, so:

Example 2 – correct: "Joey, I gave you *fewer* meatballs than Timmy because you're a human f*cking garbage disposal!" (Ma offered to give Joey another meatball, and you can just imagine where she wanted to put it. You don't mess with Ma!)

Exceptions

Now, let's be clear… the above rule will cover 99% of instances of *less* vs. *fewer*. So if you simply stick to that, you'll appear much smarter than you really are. ;-)

Just know there are some exceptions, which I won't go into here because they fall into the 1%, but if you really want to twist your brain into a pretzel, do a web search using this: "Less vs. Fewer, Time, Distance, Money, Weight." As you read about this exception, you'll appreciate my unique attempt at simplicity in this book.

On to simpler shit!

Many vs. Much

Let's make this one super easy: *many* vs. *much* is the same rule as *fewer* vs. *less*.

<u>The 99% rule</u>: Use *many* with things you can count, and *much* with things you can't.

It's that simple, folks, so stop saying the English language has too *much* confusing rules. It doesn't. It has too *many* confusing rules. (If you really want to, you can count them!)

Do you really need more examples for this one? You shouldn't, but here are a couple anyway.

> **Example 1 – wrong:** "My mother put too *much* peas on my plate." I know this is wrong because I hate peas, and my mother always said, "just eat three more," so I know you can count them.

> **Example 1 – correct:** "My mother put too *many* peas on my plate." Now that I can decide for myself, I haven't had a pea in years! (There's an old dad joke about that somewhere.)

Remember, it's things you *can* count vs. things you *can't*. For instance, you can't count gas, but you can count farts.

> **Example 2 – correct:** "Eating her homemade Rochette's Famous Beans gave me too *much* gas, so I've been ripping too *many* farts." (If you haven't tried Rochette's Famous Beans you need to. You can find the recipe online, and I adapted it to an easy crockpot recipe. Once you make them, you'll understand this sentence!)

Number and *amount* **follow the same rule:** Use *number* for things you can count and *amount* for things you can't. Sticking with the above theme: "The *number* of farts expelled is directly dependent on the *amount* of egg salad I eat."

23

Preface to the "5 Words" Chapters

This is a short preface to the various "5 Words" chapters in this book.

There are certain words people totally f*ck up, and it makes them sound less intelligent than they probably are. Unfortunately, there are *many words* that get messed up and *many people* who mess them up. And those who make these mistakes typically do it their entire lives because nobody ever corrects them.

There are too many of these words for a single chapter, so I've spread them out over multiple chapters because people learn better when information is presented in smaller chunks... and also because I don't want to destroy too many egos. ;-)

The words in the "5 Words" chapters are all examples that, to me, indicate someone doesn't read very much. But now that you're reading this book, we can fix that together. Through the various "5 Words" chapters you can finally *Smarten the F*ck Up!*

By the way, I know lots of very smart people who struggle with some of these mistakes. So if I offer you a free copy of this book, you're probably one of them. Please know I'm only trying to help.

So, on to the first of the many "5 Words" chapters!

Five Words That Make You Sound Like a Blathering Nincompoop!

For those who need to know, it's the bold instance of each word that's correct:

1. Expecially vs. **Especially:** Do people who say *expecially* think it means *extra* special? Or maybe it's just the opposite, and they're referring to something that used to be special but isn't any more, so it's *ex-special*? Whatever the reason, there's no *x* in *especially*!

2. Supposably vs. **Supposedly:** "She *supposably* taught English, yet her grammar and spelling sucked!" The word to use here is *supposedly*, which means "allegedly" or "assumed to be true" (and is now often accompanied by a sarcastic winky-face on social media). This is a very common mistake, but now you know better! I also have to mention that *supposably* is actually a word in American English, even though the British refuse to accept it. It just doesn't mean the same thing as *supposedly*, and almost every time it's used, it's a mistake. Just avoid it completely so you don't sound like a lunkhead.

3. Acrossed vs. **Across:** "She threw the dictionary at me from *acrossed* the room whenever I said *expecially*." Let's keep this one simple: *acrossed* is not a word. Neither is *acrosst*. Just say, "She threw the dictionary at me from *across* the room whenever I said *expecially*." ...and know that you deserved it!

4. Impordant vs **Important:** If you're saying something *impordant*, then it's *important* to get it right! There are a handful of TV news personalities, including several on CNN, who say *impordant* all the time. *It drives me crazy!* Here's a tip for them: do an internet search for *"important definition"* and the click on the little audio icon in the results. Then presto... you get the correct pronunciation! To the CNN personalities: I'm surprised your producer hasn't told you this already, but there's no *d* sound in *important*.

27

5. Warsh vs. **Wash:** This one is more of a regional thing, but that makes it no less cringeworthy. The U.S. has various dialects, and *warsh* is an old carryover from one called the Midland dialect. This pronunciation is disappearing... thank God! Just to be crystal clear, there's no *r* in *wash*. I've also heard lots of people say *warter* – even on national TV infomercials. There's no *r* in the middle of *water*, either.

It's vs. Its

The use of *it's* vs. *its* only matters in writing, since we don't pronounce the apostrophe. ;-)

It's is one of those darned things called a *contraction*. That may seem like a big word for some people (especially those who hold high political office), but it just refers to a single word made out of two words by replacing some letters with an apostrophe.

The rule: **The word *it's* (with an apostrophe) is a contraction for *it is*, while *its* is the possessive form of *it*. If you're not sure whether you've used the correct one, just try substituting *it is* and you'll know.**

Pretty simple, huh?

The reason so many people screw this one up is because we usually use an *'s* (apostrophe+s) to indicate possession – who something belongs to. For example, if the food belongs to the dog, we'd say, "Jimmy mistakenly ate the *dog's* food and liked it!" (I actually did this once; it was in an open container in the fridge and looked delicious.)

The *'s* on the word *dog* indicates that the food belongs to the dog. But the contraction *it's* – even though it has an *'s* – has nothing to do with posession. *It's* is always a contraction of *it is*, while *its* – without an apostrophe – is used to indicate possession. So, to restate this example I could say, "The dog explained that Jimmy mistakenly ate *its* food, and that's why it bit him."

Here are a few more sentences to illustrate the rule:

> **Example 1 – wrong:** "*Its* better to ask forgiveness than permission, unless you're robbing a bank."

To see whether you've used the correct version, simply replace *its* with *it is*. You'll see that you should have used *it's*, because "*It is* better to ask forgiveness than permission, unless you're robbing a bank." (Also, bank tellers are typically detail-oriented people and appreciate good grammar, so make sure your note is well-written.)

> **Example 2 – correct**: "After consuming an entire bowl of salsa at Margaritas Mexican Restaurant, he realized *it's* best to never trust a fart."

If you substitute *it is* for *it's* you'll see that this statement is correct, and *it is* never a good idea to trust a fart – especially after Mexican food!

> **Example 3 – wrong**: "As I was lying on the beach, the dog lifted *it's* leg as it appeared to stop to say hello."

Again, if you replace *it's* with *it is* you'll see that the correct word is *its*, meaning it was the dog's leg, and this sentence is wrong... on multiple levels.

Remember: Use *its*, not *it's*, unless *it is*!

They're, There, and Their

They're, there, and *there* are homophones – words that sound the same but have different meanings. *Homo* means same, and *phone* means sound. This is another example where you'd only come across as a dumbass when writing, for instance, in social media comments. As a matter of fact, that's where I most often find it – and it's everywhere!

Of all the mistakes covered in this book, this is one of the most egregious, yet one of the simplest to correct. Warning: my language reflects my level of (totally appropriate!) frustration. ;-)

The rule: *They're, there,* and *their* are three separate f*cking words!

1. *They're* is a contraction of "they are." That's all it means... ever!
2. *Their* refers to "something that belongs to someone." That's all it means... ever!
3. *There* is the more versatile of the three words. You can look it up to see every possible use, but in general it refers to:
    a. At, in, or to a place or position, as in "It's over there," or "She's in there," "We went there." *This represents 99% of its use.*

So, to fix 99% of this problem, if it's not *they're* or *their*, use *there*.

Would you ever confuse *earn* with *urn*? How about *die* with *dye*? Or *knows* with *nose*? You probably wouldn't, because *they're* (they are) all separate words, just like *they're, there,* and *their.*

I'm confident you can get this one right from now on, so there's no more to be said here. Just use your noggin and stop f*cking it up!

Rant over.

To vs. Too vs. Two

To, *too*, and *two* are another set of homophones: words that sound the same but have different meanings.

You can't possibly screw them up when you're speaking, but *to* many of us there are *too* many people who screw up the first *two* words when writing.

Let's start with *two* because it's the easiest: it's the number 2. *That's it. It's that simple.* The word *two* means absof*ckinglutely nothing else! *Two* is always just a number... like your age. Now let's move on to the real source of confusion.

To vs. too

Using *to* vs. *too* is where most of the mistakes are made. Luckily, using *too* is fairly simple, so let's learn that word, and then by the process of elimination all other uses will be the word *to*.

Using *too*:

Too has just *two* meanings: "also" and "excessively."

Examples with *too*, meaning *also*:

Example 1: "I bought my brother a copy of this book because he needs to *Smarten the F*ck Up*, *too*. It hit the back of the door as I left his office."

Example 2: "Someone had just blamed a fart on the dog, so Jimmy farted, *too*, thinking he had some cover, but unfortunately, his wasn't silent."

Examples with *too*, meaning *excessively*:

Example 1: "It took *too* many brain cells for Billy to comprehend that there are three different words all pronounced the same. He wasn't an avid reader and could still only recite the alphabet in song."

Example 2: "Unfortunately, Jimmy had *too* much gas to hold back when his wife, Kim, bent down behind him to pick up the fork she had dropped." (Ah, I remember it well. Everyone laughed and appreciated the exquisite timing – except Kim. And Jimmy slept on the couch that night 'cause it wasn't just his timing that stunk.)

And finally, the *to* to end them all:

The word *to* is very versatile. It can represent a direction or destination, as in:

Example 1: "I'm going *to* Walmart." (Or "I'm going *down to the* Walmart," as those who frequent the store are known to say.)

It can also represent a relationship between things, as in:

Example 2: "I watched in amazement as the dog that belonged *to* my oblivious neighbor crapped on my shoe while we talked at my mailbox."

It can also define a period of time, such as:

Example 3: "Bubba was in the bathroom for 45 *to* 50 minutes before he flushed, and, although we were all glad he was still alive, no one dared enter after he exited and put the Sunday morning paper on the table with a grin of total satisfaction."

If you replace *to* in any of the above sentences with *also* or *excessively* (the definition of *too*), you'll see that it just doesn't fit, and that the correct word is *to*.

The bottom line:
1. *Two* is a number. Period.
2. *Too* is only used when you mean "also" or "excessively".
3. In all other instances, use *to*.

You can be sure there's a grammar-nerd explanation for all of this, but just following this rule will certainly achieve the goal of this book, which is to make you 99% smarter!

Versus vs. Verse

Hearing someone say *verse* (words in poetry or song) when they mean *versus* (against) screws me into the ceiling... figuratively. (We'll come to the use of figuratively in a later chapter.)

When someone commits the sin of saying *verse* instead of *versus*, their penance should be to read poetry (or song lyrics) until they get it, because that's the only place they'll find a f*cking verse! In fact, reading more of anything (other than your friends' social media posts) would be a good cure for most maladies in this book.

I'm talkin' to you!

The hosts of sports radio and TV shows – and their guests – are the biggest abusers of this one. Whenever they say *verse* instead of *versus*, I reflexively yell at the radio or TV. Yes, I'm talking to you ESPN, CBS Sports, NBC Sports, and FOX Sports. You're all guilty!

Some sports broadcast personalities are smart enough to know the difference, and to them I say, "Thank you. Now please share this chapter with your co-workers!"

For those who don't know the difference, THIS is a verse:
You can say "v." for versus
Write "vs." for versus, too,
But this is a fucking verse, so
Don't ever confuse the two!

And *verses* simply means more than one verse. It's still not the correct word, which is *versus*!

On the next page is a simple exercise I developed specifically for sports broadcasters. It has 10 ways to help you remember the correct word. Just read each line carefully and out loud, preferably on air (so you can help your listeners, too):

39

1. It's versus, NOT verse, you dimwitted dumbass!
2. It's versus, NOT verse, you idle-brained idiot!
3. It's versus, NOT verse, you duckbill-face dickhead!
4. It's versus, NOT verse, you arrogant asshole!
5. It's versus, NOT verse, you fatheaded f*ck face!
6. It's versus, NOT verse, you Einstein imposter!
7. It's versus, NOT verse, you thin-lipped dickweed!
8. It's versus, NOT verse, you lunkheaded lug nut!
9. It's versus, NOT verse, you imbecilic f*ckbrain!
10. It's versus, NOT verse, you sapheaded shit-for-brains!

Sorry for the rant, but I feel better now. Can you tell I'm a bit sensitive about this one?

So just remember… when you're talking about one team competing against another, it's *versus! Verse* doesn't mean *against*, and it never, ever f*cking will!

Often vs. OfTen
& Other Silent Letters

The *t* in *often* is a silent letter

This mistake has grown to epidemic – maybe even pandemic – proportions. The number of people who are screwing it up is almost beyond control, but maybe this book can help turn the tide and bring the pronunciation back to where it belongs. It's been mispronounced so *ofTen* that some people are even saying it's acceptable... but it's not!

Merriam-Webster lists the *t* as non-standard pronunciation, although they include it in their audio samples. I want to be clear on this: *it's a "non-standard" pronunciation, not an alternative one.*

Many say that pronouncing the *t* in *often* is another example of people using hypercorrection, because they think it sounds more formal – similar to people saying, "between you and *I*" when they should say "between you and *me*." It's not more formal, and it doesn't make you sound more intelligent.

Here's an easy way to remember the correct pronunciation: How do you say the word *soften*? Exactly! You would NEVER pronounce the *t* in *soften*. That's how you pronounce *often*... without the *t*.

You'd also never pronounce the silent *t* in the words *listen, hasten,* or *fasten*... or the silent *l* in *salmon, half* or *would*. Try it and see just how stupid it sounds.

By pronouncing it with a silent *t*, you'll never create a "silent cringe," so stick with the correct, traditional pronunciation of *often*. And remember what your mother always said... "If all your friends jumped off a bridge, would you do it, too?" Just because many others say it doesn't make it right.

The first step in fixing a problem is awareness. *You are now aware!*

Now, I have to say that, by far, *often* seems to be the most abused of all the words with silent letters. But while we're on the subject, let's talk about them a bit because lots of words have silent letters.

Would you ever pronounce the 'd' in *Wednesday*? Of course, you wouldn't. You'd sound like an idiot... any day of the week!

Some silent letters are at the beginning of the word, as in *knife* or *write*. Try pronouncing them with the silent letter included. See? It sounds pretty stupid, and it's difficult to say, too!

There are also silent letters at the end of words, as in *solemn*, *comb*, or *faux*. And then there are other words where the silent letters are very *subtle*. (See what I did there?) ;-)

Sometimes silent letters are contained *within* the word, as in *receipt*, *rendezvous*, *sriracha* (one of my favorite sauces), *raspberry*, and *often!* Just know that if you're one of those people who pronounce the *t* in *often*, there are a bunch of people who immediately feel the silent cringe. I'm not saying their judgment is right, but you should know it happens.

Here's a tip: If you're ever not sure how to pronounce a word correctly, do an internet search by typing the *word* followed by *definition*, like this:

In the search bar type: *often definition*

You'll get results from several dictionary sources and each will have a little speaker icon (or two). Click on that icon and it'll pronounce the word for you. Check several different dictionary sources. I've noticed that a few are beginning to include non-standard pronunciations, mainly to point out the mistake because there are so many people saying it incorrectly. *Don't be one of them... please!*

And, if after reading this chapter you still think it's okay to pronounce certain silent letters, to that I say, "Bologna!"

Should, Could, Would & Might...
with Have vs. Of

Let me say this right up front: *should of, could of, would of,* and *might of* are all wrong. They make no sense at all, and anyone who knows better immediately questions the intelligence of anyone who uses these phrases. *Please don't let this happen to you!*

This common mistake comes from people misunderstanding the pronunciation of the contraction for each of these phrases, which are *should've (should have), could've (could have), would've (would have)* and *might've (might have)*.

What this mistake says to me – as do many of the mistakes in this book – is that people who use *of* instead of *have* have never stepped into the pages of a book, or even a reputable website.

If all you read is stuff written by idiots, you'll sound like an idiot. And that advice goes well beyond grammar!

If I Was vs.
If I Were

Another very common mistake (yes, I'm repeating myself) is this specific use of *was* vs. *were*. Most people don't even think about it as it comes out of their mouth because it's so widely misused that typically no one notices, but there's actually a pretty simple rule.

<u>The rule</u>: Use *was* in statements that are *factual* and *were* in statements that are *unreal* or *hypothetical*.

Here's a good clue to keep in mind: if you use the words *if* or *wish*, you should use the word *were*, since *if* and *wish* are typically used in statements that don't describe reality.

> **Example 1 – correct – using *wish*:** "I wish I *were* smarter so I wouldn't have to read this book." See what I mean? You *wish* you were smarter, but you're not. That's why you're here reading the simplest grammar book in the world. Therefore, this example doesn't describe reality… yet! But if you keep reading it will. ;-)

> **Example 2 – correct – using *if*:** "If I *were* you, I wouldn't go around pointing out people's grammar mistakes all day long." Again, you're not me so this statement doesn't describe reality.

> **Example 3 – correct:** "I *was* sitting on the toilet when the auto-flush went off and it exploded unexpectedly." This is a true story, so the word to use is *was*. The rest of this story isn't fit for a book on grammar, though.

Pretty simple, huh? Now you can start correcting others with confidence!

Five Words That Make You Sound Like a Dumb Crumbwumple

Reminder... the bold word is the correct one.

1. Reconize vs. **Recognize:** Breaking news – there IS a *g* in *recognize*... and it's not silent! You might say "Gee, I never knew that!" Remember the *g* and say it out loud.

2. Jewlery vs. **Jewelry:** Can you say *jewel*? That's what *jewelry* is made of... *jewels!* That's why it's pronounced *jewel-ry*. Pretty simple, huh? And someone who makes the stuff is called a jeweler, pronounced *jewel-er*. I've heard national ads for jewelers that mispronounce this one.

3. Expresso vs. **Espresso:** There's no *x* in *espresso*. It's typically those who don't enjoy a nice *espresso* who misstate its name, making it painstakingly obvious that they've never had one!

4. Pockabook vs. **Pocketbook:** I recently saw a manly-man carrying a *pocketbook* into Home Depot... draped over his shoulder and all. I jokingly complimented him on it and saw the immediate look of embarrassment as a wry smile appeared on his face. He removed the slender, feminine-looking strap from his shoulder upon entering the store and immediately handed it to his wife, who was waiting at the register. He then gave me the man-to-man look and subtle nod that we both understood to say, "I was being a gentleman and getting it for my wife." She erupted in laughter when she saw what had happened. At least he didn't call it a *pockabook*. Get it right, people! (This is a true story!)

5. Vetran vs. **Veteran:** This is one of many words that people *remove* a syllable from. It has three syllables, folks, not two. It's pronounced *vet-er-an*. After finishing this book you'll be a *Smarten the F*ck Up* vet-er-an! (This point also applies to *veterinarian*.)

Who's vs. Whose

Who's and *whose* are yet another example of homophones – words that sound the same but have different meanings.

The rule: *Who's* is a contraction for *who is* or *who has*. *Whose* is the possessive of *who*, meaning the person to *whom* the thing belongs.

From my experience, most people don't even know the word *whose* exists. That's why it's f*cked up so often. But deciding between *who's* and *whose* is very simple: just undo the contraction *who's* into its two words, either *who is* or *who has*, and say the sentence again.

> **Example 1 – correct:** "I asked my wife *whose* truck was leaving the driveway as I was coming home."

If you replace *whose* with *who is* or *who has* in this example you can clearly see that using *who's* doesn't make sense, so the correct version, *whose*, was used.

> **Example 2 – correct:** "She said, 'It was the electrician, *who's* been on your list to call for the last two years. I finally had the ceiling fan installed!'"

In this example, if you replace *who's* with *who has* you can see that *who's* is correct.

From this sentence you can also learn that if you make your wife wait long enough, she'll figure out how to get shit done on her own. And, as many of you know, waiting two years for a guy to complete a home project really isn't that long. I really don't understand what she was so upset about. ;-)

Your vs. You're

The word *you're* is another of those tricky contractions that seem to be a common source of confusion. And *your* is a totally different word.

The rule: *Your* means *it belongs to you*. *You're* is a contraction for *you are*.

Although this is a super-simple mistake to fix, it's another of the big ones people make on social media. I'm sure some of you get this one right and are saying, "F*ck yeah... I see this one all the time and I just don't get how people can screw it up!" If so, please help your friends get it right. The easiest way is to drop a link to this book on their comment when you see this mistake. ;-)

Seriously though, I'm not so much trying to sell books as trying to eliminate the collective frustration of those of us whose blood pressure takes a minor spike when we read this shit on social media.

My wife saw this mistake on the post of a teacher friend and I swear it made her head spin like Linda Blair in the Exorcist... and she used the same language too. (Look that one up: "Linda Blair Exorcist" and make sure you watch the video clip!)

Granted, I'll admit that when I'm typing fast (and believe me, fast is all relative, folks) I occasionally type *your* instead of *you're*, but then I re-read everything before posting and correct myself. This re-reading adds a slight pause that can even be helpful in other ways, too... like when I'm typing something I shouldn't say, which happens way too often. How many of us delete a post the morning after a few beers?

Let me add one more thing about *your*: the possessive form NEVER has an *'s*. It's always spelled *yours*. As in, "This mistake is *yours* to own."

If *your/you're* ever not sure which one to use, simply replace the word with the uncontracted version – *you are* – and it'll be obvious. Consider the difference between "your toast" vs. "you're toast". Got it? Just expand the contraction!

And speaking of contractions, don't ever mistake the pain caused by misusing grammatical contractions with those of a woman giving birth. The misuse of grammatical contractions is *much* more painful for those who witness them! ;-)

A vs. An

Just a heads up… this is probably one of the more grammar-nerdish chapters, so you may have to come back to it a few times. If it gets to be too much, just skip it. There's lots more to learn.

You can sound like a 3-year-old and say, "I want *a* apple," or you can learn the simple rule, which is:

The rule: If it comes before a word, acronym, or abbreviation that begins with a *vowel sound*, use *an*. Before a *consonant sound*, use *a*.

So, if you don't want to sound like a 3-year-old, you'd say, "I want *an* apple." But you could use *a* if you changed the sentence slightly, to "I want *a* f*cking apple." You might get what you want either way, although I wouldn't encourage teaching a 3-year-old to use the latter.

Before we continue, here's a refresher on vowels and consonants for those who need it: *vowels are a, e, i, o, u,* and sometimes *y. Every other letter is a consonant.*

The key is whether the word following *a* or *an* has a vowel or consonant *sound.* This gets a bit grammar-nerdish, but the examples below should help.

First, a brief explanation: Some words start with a consonant, but have a *vowel sound,* and some start with a vowel, but have a *consonant sound.* You have to ignore what the first letter is and listen to its *sound.* Use your best judgment, and in no time at all you'll get the hang of identifying *vowel sounds* vs. *consonant sounds.* It's easier than you think!

With that said, let's have some fun. Here are examples of *a* and *an,* all taken from actual comments on political posts I saw on social media today (FYI... none of these was directed at me):

Examples: before words that start with a *vowel* and have a *vowel sound*:

The *vowel sound* requires *an.*

Example 1: "You're *an* asshole."

Example 2: "He's *an* out-of-control idiot."

Example 3: "You're *an* anti-American regressive socialist." (OMG... what an insult! I bet this person is a grammar nerd.)

Examples: before words that start with a *consonant* and have a *consonant sound*:

The *consonant sound* requires *a.*

Example 1: "He's *a* loser."

Example 2: "He's *a* climate change denier."

Example 3: "You have *a* small penis and should STFU!"

These are actual comments folks! I didn't make them up. People say things online that they would never say face-to-face. What is this world coming to?

Examples: before words that start with a *consonant* but have a *vowel sound* (these are not actual comments from social media):

Both these examples use words that start with the (silent) consonant *h* and are pronounced using the vowel sound of the letter *o.*

Example 1: "Fred said, 'It was *an* honor to win the farting contest with so many qualified participants entered!'" Use *an* because *honor* is pronounced with the vowel sound of the letter *o*, as in "on".

Example 2: "His best one came *an* hour into the competition and caused all of the other participants to concede." (After he cleaned up, he claimed the trophy.) Use *an* because *hour* is pronounced with the vowel sound of the letter *o*, as in "our."

Examples: before words that start with a *vowel* but have a *consonant sound*:

Both of these examples use words that start with a vowel – *u* and *o* – but are pronounced using consonant sounds of the letters *y* and *w*.

Example 1: "He is *a* useless piece of shit!" Use *a* because *useless* is pronounced with the consonant sound of the letter *y*, as in "yoo." (Also, I really never understood the point of this expression because isn't every piece of shit useless?)

Example 2: "He told her it was *a* one-time lapse in judgment. She left him wondering when she responded with, 'Well, now we're even!'" Use *a* because *one* is pronounced with the consonant sound of the letter *w*, as in "won".

Using *a* and *an* with acronyms

I'm including this because so many people sound like idiots when using acronyms, and I don't want that to happen to you. For example, sports talk radio and TV people let acronyms fly off their tongue constantly. I cringe when one of them says (even years after it happened), "It's *a* NFL rule and Brady got caught," when they *should* say, "It's *an* NFL rule, and Brady did nothing that other quarterbacks haven't done for years." The letter *N* is pronounced *en*, which starts with a vowel sound, so the correct word is *an*.

Speaking of rules, here's the rule for using *a* and *an* with acronyms: When used at the beginning of an acronym these letters – all consonants – have vowel sounds because they're pronounced as individual letters. Because they have *vowel sounds*, they're preceded by *an*: F (eff), H (ach), L (el), M (em), N (en), R (arr), S (ess), and X (ex).

Examples: Using *a* and *an* with acronyms:

Here's one set of examples:

- "He's *an* NBA All Star."
- "He got *an* STD after the game."
- "Now he has *an* RX to hide from his wife."
- "She knew better, and now he's *an* EX."

And here's another:

- "She has *a* BS in English and her starting salary as a teacher is $40K per year."
- "Her friend has *an* EE degree and started at $80K per year."
- "It doesn't take *a* PhD to see that it's a f*cking shame how teachers are so under-valued."

Listening for the vowel sound might seem challenging at first, but before long it'll become second nature… like riding a bike!

And that wraps up this chapter. Wasn't it *an* interesting one? Now you have no excuse for sounding like *a* 3-year-old!

The [thuh] vs. The [thee]

Many people don't seem to make the distinction between the two pronunciations of *the*: *[thuh]* and *[thee]*. I learned this in grammar school, so it comes naturally to me. The rule is the same as in the previous chapter on *a* vs. *an,* which is:

<u>The rule</u>: When *the* precedes a word starting with a *vowel sound* it's pronounced *[thee],* otherwise, it's pronounced *[thuh].*

Not using this rule makes you sound less refined. In my opinion, it's a rule everyone should follow if they don't want to sound like a third grader. (Yes, this is my book, and I can have opinions on things like this.)

Here are some incorrect examples a third grader might use:

Example 1 – wrong: "I ate a worm in *the [thuh]* apple."

Example 2 – wrong: "I looked it up on *the [thuh]* internet to see if I would get sick."

Example 3 – wrong: "It said to take a bite from *the [thuh]* other side and keep eating, because an apple a day keeps the doctor away."

If you use this pronunciation *[thuh],* people who know better will definitely think you missed a few lessons in grammar school. They'll also look at you in a slightly different light… especially for not just throwing the apple away!

(NOTE: For a simpler, more detailed explanation on vowel sounds you can go back to the chapter on "A vs. An.")

While many people tend to always pronounce *the* as *[thuh]*, here are examples of words with *vowel sounds* where *the* should be pronounced *[thee]*. Practice these to get it right!

Using *the* pronounced as *[thee]*:

The phonetic spelling in these examples is used for illustrative purposes only.

Examples: followed by the vowel sound a: "*[Thee]* assignment the teacher gave the students – asking them to place *[thee]* apostrophe in the correct position – showed *[thee]* apathy that high school seniors have for mastering English." (She decided to use this book as the textbook for the semester!)

Examples: followed by the vowel sound e: "*[Thee]* entire class got at least half of the ten grammar questions wrong, with *[thee]* excuses ranging from 'I depend on my phone for that' to '*[Thee]* ellipsis threw me off because it involved math.'"

Examples: followed by the vowel sound i: "*[Thee]* internet has become a place where *[thee]* individual seeking the truth must determine which sources to trust for *[thee]* information." (And it never comes from some asshole ranting on YouTube!)

Examples: followed by the vowel sound o: "*[Thee]* only thing to fear is fear itself, unless *[thee]* odor you smell is dripping out of the baby's diaper as you bounce her on your knee. That's *[thee]* other thing to fear!"

Examples: followed by the vowel sound u: "*[Thee]* Uber driver ignored *[thee]* urgent nature of their request to stop the car for their 3-year-old, and *[thee]* utter dismay was evident on his face when he saw the wet spot as they exited his car."

The above examples are all vowels with a *vowel sound*. But just as with *a* and *an*, when a word that starts with a vowel doesn't keep the *vowel sound*, use *[thuh]*. For example, we pronounce *the* as *[thuh]* with *the* United States, *the* ukulele, *the* URL, as they all begin with a consonant y sound, as in *you*.

You can also use what's called the "emphatic the" – pronounced *[thee]* – whether or not the word begins with a consonant or vowel sound. For example, "Officer, this is honestly *the [thee]* first time I have ever run a stop sign!"

Bring vs. Take

You've gotta love the easy ones, like *bring* vs. *take*. (This chapter pertains to the definition of each word that refers to moving or possessing an object.)

<u>The rule</u>: You bring something to a place, and you take something away. (That's the *takeaway* from this rule!)

So, you're right to bring it with you when you come; but you take it with you when you go.

How simple is that!!!

For instance, we all *bring* shit into a relationship and *take* shit from it. Some of us even *take* shit *within* a relationship. (This book is only about your relationship with the English language, so we're not going to talk about that other stuff.)

Here are a couple of simple examples:

> **Example 1 – using bring:** She said, "When I go to a party, I always *bring* one bottle of wine for the host and one for myself... although I usually end up drinking both of them!"

> **Example 2 – using take:** "Please *take* the garbage to the dump, and don't leave it in the back of your car this time. It's going to be 95 degrees today!"

It can't be much simpler than that!

Redundant Words (Synonym Rolls)

"Whole entire," "big huge," "exact same," "tiny little" – these are all pairs of redundant synonyms that people often string together. Once you realize you're using them, you begin to notice that you sound like a 5-year-old at show-and-tell.

If you're using redundant synonyms for emphasis, the only thing you're emphasizing is that you don't really understand the meaning of each word. So, to prevent a synonym roll you might want to eat some of your words.

Lots of people have this habit, so don't feel bad. But now that you know better you can have fun pointing it out when others do it. You'll be the life of the party, until someone punches you in the face. ;-)

Changing this habit is pretty tough, though... especially in a moment of excitement! For instance, some people I've corrected have yelled at me, saying, "You act as if it's a big huge mistake, asshole!" And other people just don't give a shit. I get that reaction all the time. They're probably the ones who say they *could care less* (there's a chapter on that), which shows how much they could benefit from reading this book, but they'd probably never buy a copy.

Here are some common examples of redundant words to avoid so others don't think you work for the Department of Redundancy Department:

Whole entire: The word *whole* literally means *entire*.

Exact same or **same identical:** These words mean the *exact* or *same* thing! ;-)

Big huge or **big giant:** Some male friends of mine would love to be defined using these redundant attributes, but we go to the same gym, so not only are these words redundant, they're inaccurate. Sorry, Tim! ;-)

Tiny little: Again, they mean the same thing. NO male friends of mine would ever want to hear these redundant words used to describe them, although I'm sure some have. They've probably also heard the words "cute little," and, although this phrase is not redundant, I still don't think they'd find it very complimentary!

Free gift: All gifts are free... unless they're offered in an infomercial (one way or another, you always pay for everything offered in an infomercial). That's what they mean when they say, "But wait! Just pay a separate fee and we'll double your order!" (I'll bet you just read that in an infomercial voice.)

Close proximity: A lot of people use the word *close* before *proximity* because they don't know what *proximity* means. It means you're close! Another duh moment!

Prediction about the future: Umm... every prediction is about the future.

Adequate enough: Adequate means good enough! I hope this explanation is adequate.

Ask a question: Would you ever ask a statement? No, it's always a question. Just say, "Can I ask you about..."

All-time record: That's what a record is... the best of all time. It's just a f*cking record. That's it!

Revert back: Revert means *to go back to*. You'd never revert forward, right?

Brief moment: That's what a moment is... brief. If you're referring to a situation where a hot guy exposed his underwear, then that may very well be described as a "brief moment," but otherwise it's redundant.

Reason why: Like most of these, it's intuitively obvious to the most casual observer that the phrase is totally redundant. The word *reason* means *why*. The reason I point this out is so you'll never sound stupid again by saying "The reason why I point this out is..."

ATM machine: The "M" in ATM stands for "machine," so would you ever say, "Automated Teller Machine Machine"? No, of course you wouldn't. So just *Smarten the F*ck Up!*

There are lots more, but you get the idea. Just do an internet search for "redundant words and phrases" and you'll find other ways you can avoid sounding stupid. ;-)

Using an Ellipsis...

Ellipsis = …

Let me start by saying that an ellipsis is always 3 periods, PERIOD! Lots of people get this one wrong, but it's easy as 1, 2, 3… periods.

Most people don't even know what an ellipsis is, but they use them – *incorrectly* – all the time… especially on social media! (See what I did there?)

Important: For the grammar nerds reading this, before you get yourself all twisted into a shit-knot, here's my ellipsis-use disclaimer: For the purpose of this book, I'm referring to the informal use of ellipsis on social media and in text messages and email.

When you use an ellipsis, please don't just hold down the period key until you think you've got enough of them. If you're smart enough to count to three, you're smart enough to use an ellipsis correctly.

And don't put a space before it, but most definitely put one after it… unless you're using punctuation such as a question mark or exclamation point to end your sentence or comment. Should I show you how…? Yes, I should…!

The term ellipsis (plural: ellipses) comes from a Greek word that means "to leave out" or "to omit." In *formal* writing it's used to indicate there are words that are omitted. In *informal* writing – as on social media – it's also used to indicate a pause in speech, suspense, mystery, hesitation, or that a thought trails off.

As I mentioned, this chapter focuses on the *informal* use of the ellipsis, such as:

- To elicit a response
- To indicate that you're about to say more
- When you're suggesting something

It's pretty f*cking versatile, huh? For instance, here are some simple examples of using what I'll call the *social media ellipsis*:

- "He invited you in for a drink? And...?"
- "So...?"
- "I know you said I should be there by 2:00, but..."
- "I wish you'd just come over so we could..."

Here's an interesting tidbit: I thought ellipses were only used in writing until I heard a friend say "dot, dot, dot" at the end of a statement. I guess that's becoming a thing! Who would have thought social media lingo would migrate into verbal conversation... LOL!

For the wannabe grammar nerds, here's the formal use of an ellipsis:

An ellipsis in formal writing is typically used to eliminate words from a direct quote. When words in a quote don't add substantive content, they can be replaced with an ellipsis to make the quote more concise. For instance, if you use one to eliminate words in the middle of a direct quote you would replace the removed words with an ellipsis and add a space on each side. For example:

Example – full quote: "The chapter on ellipses is my favorite one because I really like it, and the 5-word chapters are cool, too."

Example – edited quote: "The chapter on ellipses is my favorite ... and the 5-word chapters are cool, too."

If you want a more detailed explanation on the use of an ellipsis, you can look it up. You'll find a variety of rules on its use in formal writing. Things like putting spaces between each period, adding a fourth period when it's used at the end of a sentence, along with other rules and disagreements that prove grammar nerds can be the life of the party!

I'll say it again... my goal here isn't to create more grammar nerds, but to make the average person a bit smarter. Do you feel a bit smarter now? Good!

Do you have a friend who abuses the ellipsis? *Smarten the F*ck Up* makes a great gift! (Sorry for the shameless plug.)

Five Words That Make You Sound Like an Ignorant Dickwinker

Reminder... the bold word is the correct one.

1. Excape vs. **Escape:** If you're a superhero who has graduated to the next level and earned a new cape, you might show someone your *ex-cape*, but if you're captured by the bad guys and get away, then it's called an *escape*. Get it right, and be a grammar superhero, too!

2. Esculate or excalate vs. **Escalate:** If you say *esculate* or *excalate* instead of *es-ca-late*, you should feel emasculated. (If you don't get it, look it up... it's a good thing to get used to.) Get it right so you don't sound like an ignorant dickwinker!

3. Axe or ax vs. **Ask:** If you *axe* someone, you'll probably end up in jail. If you have a question for someone, you *ask* it. I understand the historical background of using *ax* and I appreciate it; however, I'm dealing with the general public's perception of *you* and your use of grammar and the English language. Please don't give anyone a reason to question your intelligence – use *ask*.

4. Nucular vs. **Nuclear:** President George W. Bush was famous for mispronouncing this word. Don't be like George!

5. Perculate vs. **Percolate:** If you've ever made a pot of coffee or done a soil drainage test, you know *perculate* isn't a real word. Here's a little story: One day, I made a pot of coffee for the office. I had just poured a cup when someone came in and asked if it was done "*perculating*". I spontaneously snorted my coffee and started choking and coughing. When they asked why, I made something up because I didn't want them to feel stupid. Later I told them the truth, but only after letting the situation *percolate* a while. They know better now and we both joke about it.

Way, Shape or Form vs. Way

By now, you may have guessed that I listen to a lot of sports (and news). But I'm also interested in grammar, and, unfortunately, it's painfully obvious that sportscasters and grammar afficionados don't go to the same parties. This chapter is dedicated to all the sports talk show hosts (and some news commentators, too).

What's the difference between each word in the phrase *way, shape, or form*?

In the context where this phrase is typically used, there really is no difference. "*Way, shape, or form*" is just an over-used idiom uttered by those who want to sound smarter than they are when all they're really proving is that they don't understand the simple meaning of the word *way*. How embarrassing is that!

Here's my plea to all sports talk show hosts and news commentators: *PLEASE STOP USING THIS!* You're killing people, including me. Between this phrase and using *verse* instead of *versus*, I don't know which is more responsible for my high blood pressure, and you guys are by far the biggest abusers of both.

Adding *shape* and *form* is just an attempt to intensify the word *way*, which is totally unnecessary. If you really want to intensify the word *way*, try this: "There's no f*cking way!" How's that for an intensifier?

If you think you sound smarter by using this phrase, you don't! You sound stupider. (Yes, that's a word.)

Well vs. Good

My main reason for including *well vs. good* in this collection of common mistakes is to help people who feel stupid when answering the "How are you?" question we all encounter so often.

"How are you?" Here's the general rule:

- If you're response is regarding your health, say "I'm well."
- If your response is regarding your emotional state, say "I feel good" or "I'm good." *It's perfectly fine to say this!*

NOTE: If instead they ask, "How are you *doing*?" the answer is "I'm doing well." You *are* good, and you *are* well, but when you *do* something you do it *well*, you don't do it *good*.

Here are some general guidelines for using *well* vs. *good* in other contexts.

Grammar-speak alert! *The following goes beyond what I intended to cover in this chapter, but it's an area where mistakes are common so I'm including it. If reading this is twisting your brain into a knot, feel free to skip it.*

Using *well* vs. *good*.

- **Use *well* with verbs (actions – things people *do*).**
  The word *well* is an adverb; it's used to *describe verbs*.
- **Use good with nouns (things).**
  The word *good* is an adjective; it's used to *describe things*.

Here are some simple examples of using *well* to describe an action:

Example 1 – correct: "She sings *well*, but I'm tone deaf so what the hell would I know?" *Well* describes the action – how she *sings*. "She sings good" is wrong.

Example 2 – correct: "He runs *well*, even though he waddles like a f*cking duck." *Well* describes the action – how he *runs*. "He runs good" is wrong.

Here are some simple examples of using *good* to describe a thing:

Example 1 – correct: "He thought she was a *good* listener because she didn't talk over him, but then she took her ear buds out." (*good* describes a *thing* – the listener)

Example 2 – correct: "He ultimately regretted calling the number on the bathroom stall that said, 'For a *good* time call...'" (*good* describes a thing – the *time*)

When talking about *health*, always use *well*, which has several definitions, and in this case, means "in good health."

Example 1 – correct: "I could see he didn't look *well* just before he puked all over the floor."

Example 2 – correct: "I told my boss I wasn't feeling *well* so I could skip work and go to the baseball game on opening day."

If you're referring to someone's emotional state, use *good*.

Example 1 – correct: "She didn't feel *good* about the sarcastic comment she left on his post because she forgot to add a winky face to show she was only kidding."

Example 2 – correct: "He didn't feel *good* about who he was voting for, so he held his nose and marked an x."

I hope *Smarten the F*ck Up* is helping you learn *well* and become a *good* speaker!

Have vs. Of
with
Went vs. Gone

If you say "I *should of went* for the catfish" you might as well buy a ticket for the travellin' redneck convention 'cause you'll fit right in!

Let me point out the BIG elephant in this room first: the word *of* is NEVER used after the words *could, should,* or *would.* NEVER. EVER! The words *could of, should of,* or *would of* must never, ever leave your lips… unless you're a comedian doing a redneck skit. (Using *could of, should of,* or *would of* was covered in a previous chapter. I point it out here because these words are often used with *went* and *gone.*)

Now, on to Went vs. Gone

The most common mistake with *went* vs. *gone* happens when they are used with *has, had,* or *have.* You should NEVER use *has, had,* or *have* before the word *went. Has went, had went,* and *have went* are all embarrassingly wrong.

<u>The rule</u>: *has, had,* or *have* are used with *gone,* not *went.*

This includes the negative form too, as in *has not, had not,* or *have not,* including their contractions. The bottom line is: when using *has, had,* or *have* in any form – including as part of a contraction or in a negative sense – the correct word to use is *gone,* not *went.*

For reference, here are the ways to use *has, had,* or *have* with *gone.*

- Has, had, or have *gone*
- Has not, had not, or have not *gone*
- Hasn't, hadn't, haven't *gone*
- Could have, should have, would have *gone*
- Could've, should've, would've *gone*

- And even the controversial double contractions: couldn't've, shouldn't've, wouldn't've *gone,* even if you paid me!

Here are some examples:

Example 1 – wrong (using *went*): "She would've *went* with me but she would've been embarrassed to be seen at the redneck convention."

Example 1 – correct (using *gone*): "She would've *gone* with me if I had lied to her about where we were going."

Example 2 – correct (using *went*): "She *went* out with her friends instead and told them I *went* to a basketball game." (Reminder: Never use *has*, *had,* or *have* with *went*.)

Example 3 – correct (using *went* and *gone*): "She *went* out with her friends instead and told them I *had gone* to a basketball game."

And there you have it. You now know how to sound somewhat smarter when attending a redneck convention!

Interesting note: The term "redneck" is one lots of people poke fun at. It has different connotations for different people, but I think its origin is important to point out. The term was originally coined to describe farmers who had worked out in their fields all day in the hot sun and whose necks were sunburned. It described a hard-working man doing an important job. We should all respect rednecked farmers for what they do and for their ability to take those of us who may poke fun at them from time-to-time with a grain of salt.

I Could Care Less!

The phrase "I could care less" is almost always mistakenly used instead of "I couldn't care less." What people really mean is that they don't care about something *at all*.

99.99% of people who say "I could care less" mean "I couldn't care less."

If you remove the contraction and say the words slowly, the difference becomes obvious: "I *could not* care less" versus "I could care less." So, if you want to be crystal clear when expressing that you don't care at all, the correct phrase is "I couldn't f*cking care less!" (Using the word f*cking as an intensifier has become a substantive part of our vernacular and really drills home how little you care about whatever it is you're talking about. Don't you agree?)

Here's an analogy to help make the point: If your wife tells you where she wants to go to dinner and you love the place she suggests, would you say, "I could agree more" or "I couldn't agree more?"

To those who frequently get this one wrong, sorry, but this one takes time. Your problem won't end now that you know the difference. You'll get it wrong lots more times before you start getting it right. Think back to when you were being potty trained. Did you always make it to the toilet? No, you didn't. Sometimes you messed up – literally. You'll do that here, too. Until you get yourself "properly trained" you'll continue to mess it up. But when you finally get it right, you'll start correcting your family and friends, and that's how you'll know you've mastered it.

And if you're not comfortable correcting your family and friends, you can just take the passive-aggressive approach and buy them a copy of this book so they can *Smarten the F*ck Up*, too.

The Oxford Comma

The *Oxford comma* is also called a *serial comma*, because it's typically used to clarify words used in a series. It specifically applies to the last entry in a series, and for good reason!

Here are a few examples of how using an Oxford comma can clarify a sentence:

Example 1 – WITHOUT an Oxford comma: "While I was back in town visiting, I saw my parents, Ed Sheeran and Taylor Swift."

This sentence implies your parents are Ed Sheeran and Taylor Swift.

Example 1 – WITH an Oxford comma: "While I was back in town visiting, I saw my parents, Ed Sheeran, and Taylor Swift."

Adding the Oxford comma makes it clear that your parents aren't celebrities, but just good, honest people. Here's another example:

Example 2 – WITHOUT an Oxford comma: "My mother loves cooking, her family and her cat."

Although my mother isn't a psycho and has never cooked her family or her cat, adding the Oxford comma makes it crystal clear that there are three things my mother likes:

Example 2 – WITH an Oxford comma: "My mother loves cooking, her family, and her cat."

Here's one last example:

Example 3 – WITHOUT the Oxford comma: (This joke intro takes on a whole new meaning): "The politician, a racist and a misogynist walked into a bar."

Since we don't want to imply that the politician is a racist and a misogynist, the intro line should read:

> **Example 3 – WITH the Oxford comma:** "The politician, a racist, and a misogynist walked into a bar." (I'm sure some will say the Oxford comma isn't needed here.) ;-)

In case you skipped the Introduction, here's a good general rule to follow, and it goes well beyond the use of the Oxford comma:

As Robert Louis Stevenson once said, *"Don't write merely to be understood. Write so that you cannot possibly be misunderstood."*

This has long been one of my favorite quotes, and I mention it again here because the Oxford comma fits into that thinking. It's not always required, but as you can see, there are times when not using it can totally change the meaning of the sentence.

Here's an interesting story about the usefulness of the Oxford comma:

Not using an Oxford comma cost Oakhurst Dairy of Maine $5M when the company's drivers sued to get overtime pay. Maine's overtime law says it doesn't apply to the "canning, processing, preserving, freezing, drying, marketing, storing, packing for shipment or distribution of" foods.

Since there's no comma after "shipment", the drivers said the law referred to the activity of "packing for shipment or distribution", but they weren't doing any packing, only distribution. An Oxford comma would have made that clear. They won.

That's an expensive grammar mistake! So, follow Robert Louis Stevenson's advice. Otherwise, you might just be misunderstood in court one day!

Mute vs. Moot

Saying *mute* instead of *moot* is as dumb as mixing up the words *cute* and *coot*. Sure, they sound alike, but they're totally different words. Would you rather be a cute mute, or a moot coot? Look 'em up... it's a good habit to acquire!

The confusion between *mute* and *moot* probably comes from the fact that the words kind of sound alike, and also because the person saying "It's a *mute* point" is a lazy son-of-a-bitch and never cared to take the time to look it up to understand what the f*ck a *moot* point really is!

Mute

Definition: in general, *mute* means "to reduce or eliminate sound," or "unable to speak."

There's no such thing as a *mute* point, although I'm sure there are days when we all wish certain people would make a *mute* point and just STFU. But that's not the point of pointing out the difference between these two words. The point is to make you sound a bit smarter for reading this chapter. So, here's more....

Moot

Definition: subject to question or having no practical significance; a topic that's disputed or debatable.

When someone says it's a *moot* point, they mean it doesn't really matter or is irrelevant. It's that simple. So, even debating the validity of the phrase "*mute* point" is a *moot* point.

Five Words That Make You Sound like a Pimplebutted Idiot

Reminder (again)... the bold word is the correct one.

1. Eggsecute vs. **Execute:** Yes, eggs are cute, especially when you're taking a fresh, warm one from underneath a chicken... and especially if it's blue! While I can't say I've ever seen anyone write *eggsecute*, I've heard it pronounced this way often. There's no *egg* in *execute*!

2. 3. Alls I know vs. **All I know** – A variant on this common mistake is "Alls you need." Remember: There is never an *s* on the word *all*! Saying *"Alls I know"* will raise the eyebrows of anyone who knows better, which is most people, while saying it correctly may make you sound smarter than you really are. ;-)

3. Sherbert vs. **Sherbet:** Every time I hear someone say *sherbert* I hear the Swedish Chef on Sesame Street when Bert asks for ice cream... "Sure, Bert!" If you learn to say it correctly, it's a *sure bet* you'll always get what you want!

4. Asterick vs. **Asterisk:** The only time I use the word *asterick* is at parties when I say "Hey, check out this ass trick!" and then the room clears. But in this technology-prevalent age the word *asterisk* is becoming more necessary, especially in written communication. So, stop doing *ass tricks* and get it right!

5. Perogative vs. **Prerogative:** A lot of people use this word in conversation to sound smart. When I hear *perogative*, my mind repeats it several times in a silent, delayed, echo voice (like on a comedy TV show). Hmmm... should I correct them outright, or passive-aggressively use the correct word in responding? I usually go for the latter. It's more fun (and probably more polite, too) to leave them wondering than to leave them butt-hurt.

Accept vs. Except

Everyone has a smartphone these days. That means everyone has a dictionary, too. And it's right at your fingertips for better than 90% of the day, so if you're not sure which word to choose, simply type six letters into your smartphone! It takes just a few seconds.

If you were to look up *accept* and *except*, you'd find that they're two separate and distinct words – as different as yogurt and sex – and to misuse them indicates you're just lazy. I'll assume you still haven't looked them up for yourself (even with the intentional scolding provided above), so here are the definitions:

Accept

Definition: To say yes to something, to receive something, or to hold something as true.

> **Example:** "I *accept* that I'm a lazy SOB, and I appreciate you pointing out the difference between *accept* and *except* so I don't have to look it up myself."

Here you're *accepting* the statement by agreeing that, "Yes, I'm a lazy SOB."

Except

Definition: To exclude or leave something out.

> **Example:** "I think everyone understands the difference between these two words *except* me."

Here, you're suggesting that you're the only one who doesn't know this – you're the *exception*. We know that's not true because it's a mistake common enough to be included in this book, so you're not alone! But now you know better.

Dave Bastien

Affect vs. Effect

Okay... I agree that *affect* and *effect* can be easily confused, but I hope these simple definitions and examples resolve that. This chapter may not *affect* your intelligence but I hope the *effect* won't be to dissuade you from reading the rest of the book so you can at least somewhat *Smarten the F*ck Up*.

Affect – an *action*

Definition: *Affect* means to *impact, influence,* or *change.*

> **Example 1 – using the *impact* definition:** "He didn't think the tequila would *affect* him, but when it kicked in all he could say was 'Blah, blah, blah, blah, blah'." (This is a true example, courtesy of my brother!)

> **Example 2 – using the *influence* definition:** "We can *affect* how people perceive us by not being an asshole to them... especially when drinking tequila."

Effect – the *result* of an action

Definition: *Effect* is the *result, consequence,* or *outcome* of a change or an action.

> **Example 1 – using the *consequence* definition:** "The *effect* of the alcohol – likely shots of tequila – was to block the connection between his brain and his mouth."

> **Example 2 – using the *result* definition:** "When it comes to shots of tequila, the cumulative *effect* is often to remove inhibitions that may otherwise protect your reputation."

Drinking tequila *affects* you in a way that makes you say stupid things. That *effect* cannot be blamed on *Smarten the F*ck Up!* This book can't fix that kind of stupid. ;-)

Dave Bastien

Adverse vs. Averse

The words *adverse* and *averse* not only sound similar, but they're also both negative in meaning, which adds to the confusion. I don't think you'll ever see either of them on a "Life is Good" t-shirt!

People mix them up all the time, and lots of folks who hear them misused don't know the difference either. But with this head-to-head comparison, you'll longer be one of them. It's really not that difficult to understand the difference, so here goes:

Adverse – a negative condition or reaction

Definition: Refers to something that has negative consequences or effects, works against you, or is in opposition.

Synonyms: *unfavorable, detrimental, negative, counter, hostile.*

Exercise: To better understand the word *adverse*, simply replace its use in the example sentence below with each of the synonyms above.

> **Example:** "She had an immediate *adverse* reaction after taking a bite of the habanero pepper and, as her eyes began to water, she screamed, 'Oh my God… my f*cking mouth is on fire.'"

> When you replace *adverse* in the above sentence with each of the listed synonyms, you'll see that the intent of the sentence remains intact.

Averse – a negative feeling or attitude

Definition: Having a strong feeling of dislike, being opposed to or against. It usually applies to people, feelings, or attitudes.

Synonyms: *Disinclined, opposed, reluctant, unwilling.*

Exercise: Again, try this: To better understand the use of the word *averse*, simply replace it in the example sentence below with each of the synonyms above.

> **Example:** "She was *averse* to eating habanero peppers because of a previous morning-after reaction she once had that was just as bad as when she ate them the night before." (It renewed her appreciation for her recently installed bidet.)

I hope this synonym replacement exercise helps you better understand the difference between *adverse* and *averse,* which is easy, especially when compared to dealing with the *effects* of eating habanero peppers and how they *affect* your digestive system!

Further
vs.
Farther

This is another pair of similar words that lots of people find confusing. In general, it's acceptable to use either word, but there's a pretty easy way to remember the difference. Here's a simple rule, although it's not a strict one:

The rule: Use *further* for metaphorical or figurative distance. Use *farther* when referring to physical, measurable distance.

You can remember the difference because *farther* has the word "far" in it, and "far" relates to physical distance. So, when talking about a distance that can be measured, use *farther*; otherwise, use *further*.

This one doesn't need a lot of examples, so here's one of each:

> **Example 1 – using *further*:** "After their 22nd date, she kissed him and asked if they could go *further*." (Obviously, she's a good Catholic girl.)

> **Example 2 – using *farther*:** "He said, 'I thought you'd never ask, but I live *farther* than you, so let's go to your place."

If you're not clear about which one to use, go with *further* because it has fewer restrictions.

This topic needs no *further* explanation!

Weather vs. Whether

It's pretty obvious that this mistake can only be made in writing. *Weather* and *whether* are yet another example of homophones – words that sound the same but have different meanings. Because they sound the same, you obviously can't misuse homophones when speaking! This chapter represents the most common mistake people make when using *weather* vs. *whether*.

The word *weather* means what you see when you look outside to know if it's raining, snowing, sunny, or hot as f*cking hell. *Weather* also causes wear and tear on things, making them appear *weathered*. And surviving a storm (or any personal trying time) is also something we *weather*. *These are the only definitions of weather!*

Here's a way to remember the difference:

Weather has the letter *a* in it. The word *atmosphere* starts with the letter *a,* and weather – with an *a* – is about what's happening in the physical atmosphere, and sometimes your personal atmosphere!

If you're not talking about the weather, being worn down by the weather, or surviving a storm, use *whether*. *Whether* expresses doubt between alternatives, refers to one or more possibilities, or expresses uncertainty.

> **Example:** "I don't know *whether* or not you saw the report today, but the *weather* forecast says it's going to snow like f*ck, so you better go buy a shitload of toilet paper and beer!"

Now that you know this simple way to understand the difference between *weather* and *whether,* there's no excuse to ever make this mistake again, regardless of *whether* the *weather* is good or bad.

Don't Use No Double Negatives

Double negatives are one thing that will make you sound like you just picked your nose all the way thought English class in grammar school. If that's *snot* how you want to be seen, read on to understand how to correct this mistake so you *nose* better in the future.

Don't ever use no double negatives! (It hurt to type that.) They cancel each other out and create a positive. Here are some examples:

> **Example 1 – wrong:** "When the police asked him if he did it, he said, 'I didn't do nothin'.'"

This double negative is real trouble, because if he didn't do nothin', he did somethin'! And when the police hear someone talk like this, they think they're making up a bullshit alibi, so you'd better get this one right!

> **Example 1 – correct:** The sentence should say, "When the police asked him if he did it, he said 'I'm sorry, officer. I didn't do anything.'" (I may have just saved you a night in jail.) ;-)

Here's another example:

> **Example 2 – wrong:** When the police pull you over and ask whether you've been drinking, if you say "We didn't drink no beers tonight," you're actually telling them you had a few.

> **Example 2 – correct:** Although drinking and driving is a double negative itself, what you should be able to say is, "We didn't drink any beers tonight, officer, but thank you for asking."

Here's a good joke about double negatives:

An MIT linguistics professor was lecturing his class. "In English," he said, "a double negative forms a positive. However, in some languages, such as Russian, a double negative remains a negative. But there isn't a single language – not one – in which a double positive can express a negative." A voice from the back of the room piped up and said, "Yeah, right."

The bottom line: When it comes to double negatives, you want to be able to say, "I don't know nothin'." (And when you get this, you're ready to move on!)

Like, Um, You Know!

Like, um, you know, the first step toward fixing this is awareness.

We've all been in conversations where every other word was *"like"*, *"um"*, or *"you know"*. It's difficult to pay attention to the substance of the conversation because this habit is so distracting. If you do this – no matter how brilliant what you say may be – it makes you appear less polished or professional and diminishes the likely very smart point you were making.

Slow down!

If you have this habit, here's a simple suggestion: slow down a bit or pause before speaking. If you speak a little more slowly, or even pause now and then, your brain will find the right words and you won't need to interject *"like"*, *"um"*, and *"you know"*. Um, you'll, like, even sound smarter, you know?

The simple act of pausing before speaking has even greater benefits when it comes to preventing you from saying other stupid things… trust me on this one, I know! (This may actually be the best advice in the book!)

Here's a valuable exercise…

If slowing down or pausing is difficult for you, here's a simple exercise to help you cure this verbal malady: record a conversation with a friend and listen to it a few times. You might be embarrassed when you hear yourself speak, but this is a very effective exercise to increase your awareness, which is an important step toward fixing it. Just use a voice recorder app on your phone while you're out having a beer with a friend.

I've conducted hundreds of job interviews over the years, and have never hired anyone who repeatedly said *"like"*, *"um"*, and *"you know"*. It's an immediate red flag for many employers, especially when hiring for positions that involve interacting with customers, as mine did.

So, don't let this habit relegate your career to lower-level jobs! You can get the job you like… um, you know?

Five Words That Make You Sound Link a Jackpopping Quack

Reminder... the bold word is the correct one.

1. Perscription vs. **Prescription:** You doctor *prescribes* medication. So when you go to the pharmacy, you pick up your *prescription*. It's *p-r-e*, not *p-e-r!* Of course, you'll still have to pay per prescription.

2. Estatic vs. **Ecstatic:** Earlier I mentioned words that have silent letters... *this ain't one of 'em!* The *c* is pronounced as a *hard c* (which sounds like the letter *k*). A *soft c* would sound like the letter *s*, but this word actually has an *s* following the *c,* so if it were a *soft c* you wouldn't need it! Are you still with me? If not, that's okay. It's pronounced ec-stat-ic.

3. Orangutang vs. **Orangutan:** Yes, orangutans may seem to have a slight orange tint, but there's no *tang* in orangutan! (Do people still drink Tang?) A quick web search will tell you the correct pronunciation so the next time you're at the zoo and you say, "Look! The *orangutang* is licking himself!" you'll know why people are looking at you as if you're a complete idiot, and it'll be because you're standing right in front of the sign that says, "Orangutan Exhibit".

4. Congradulate vs. **Congratulate:** There's really not much to say about this one other than that *congradulate* isn't a f*cking word. Some people mess it up because their mind associates the pronunciation with the word *graduate*, as in "Congratulations on your graduation." Just remember... adding a *d* in congratulate is *d*umb!

5. Anyways vs. **Anyway:** This is another simple one: there's never an *s* at the end of *anyway*. If you say *anyways*, you'll sound like a 3rd grader... as is, "Go ahead, you can keep your cookies... I don't like them anyways!" (...said in a childish, sarcastic voice.)

WTF is an Eggcorn?

WTF is an eggcorn?

An eggcorn is created when you substitute a word or words in a commonly used phrase with a word or words that sound either identical or nearly identical and use it with the same intended meaning as the original phrase. This may sound a bit confusing, but as you'll see here, eggcorns are just simple, careless mistakes.

Here are some common examples:

Original: *dog-eat-dog* – Eggcorn: *doggy-dog*
Original: *row to hoe* – Eggcorn: *road to hoe*
Original: *biding my time* – Eggcorn: *biting my time*
Original: *nip it in the bud* – Eggcorn: *nip it in the butt*
Original: *it takes two to tango* – Eggcorn: *it takes two to tangle*
Original: *a scapegoat* – Eggcorn: *an escape goat*
Original: *got off scot-free* – Eggcorn: *got off scotch free*
Original: *buck naked* – Eggcorn: *butt naked*
Original: *deep-seated* – Eggcorn: *deep-seeded*
Original: *the lesser of two evils* – Eggcorn: *the lesser of two equals*
Original: *last ditch effort* – Eggcorn: *last stich effort*
Original: *as dusk fell* – Eggcorn: *as dust fell*
Original: *happy as a clam* – Eggcorn: *happy as a clown*
Original: *in the midst of things* – Eggcorn: *in the mist of things*

RANT BREAK!

I want to take this opportunity to rant a bit, because this brings to mind a larger problem with people misusing phrases, grammar, spelling, etc., which, as I've said several times before, is laziness. Laziness with regard to reading. Laziness with regard to looking up things they don't understand, especially when they have a world of information at their lazy fingertips.

I'm sure you don't want to sound stupid, but when you use words or phrases you don't understand, you will – especially when you use one of the many obvious eggcorns.

If you're even slightly unsure of the meaning or spelling of a word or phrase, there's no longer any excuse for not looking it up! These days internet-connected devices are always at your fingertips, so use them... your fingertips, that is. And if you're too lazy to type, just tap on the little f*cking microphone icon and speak into your phone to get your answer. It takes less than sixty seconds. And if you're *super* lazy, you could even use Siri or Alexa. You can just sit on your ass on the couch and talk to your phone while you have a margarita. How cool is that? There are lots of options, so there are NO MORE EXCUSES. Just use your brain, or at least your smartphone, and look it up. End of rant.

Here's a fun and helpful exercise:

Do an internet search for eggcorns and you'll find many lists of them. Scan those for a few you may have used, then take a couple of minutes to look up their meaning. It's an interesting and informative exercise. You'll see that using an obvious eggcorn makes you sound like a dumbass. Please, don't be a dumbass!

I'll end this chapter with one final eggcorn I heard recently: it's **home in**, not *hone in*. To *home in* means to move toward a destination or target. To *hone* means to sharpen, refine, or perfect.

Here's an example that uses both correctly:

"As I searched the *Smarten the F*ck Up* table of contents, I *homed in* on the areas that will help me *hone* my skills and stop sounding like an idiot."

Seen vs. Saw

In this chapter we focus on the most blatant abuse of using *seen* instead of *saw*.

When people use *seen* incorrectly, 99% of the time it's because they forgot to add one of these three words: *has, had,* or *have*.

Example – wrong: "I *seen* the light!"
Example – correct: "I *have seen* the light!"

I honestly feel bad for people who make this mistake, because I feel they were somehow deprived of a basic education. I assume they grew up in a household that struggled to make ends meet, or that somehow life was just more difficult for them.

We know that being able to speak correctly opens up more economic opportunity, and to me this mistake is an obvious sign that a good educational opportunity wasn't available. So, no poking fun at people here.

Here's how to *Smarten the F*ck Up* when using *seen* vs. *saw*:

Seen and *saw* are both verbs, meaning they both refer to action. When used in the context covered in this chapter, the word *seen*, must also include either *has, had,* or *have*. (They're called helping verbs, or auxiliary verbs for the true grammar nerds!)

Here are some examples:

Example 1 – using *have*:

Wrong: "I *seen* it on the shelf at Walmart!"
Correct: "I *have seen* it on the shelf at Walmart." You can also use the contraction for *I have*, and say, "*I've seen* it on the shelf

at Walmart."

Also correct – using saw (don't use *has, had,* or *have* with *saw*): "I *saw* it on the shelf at Walmart."

Example 2 – using *has*:

Wrong: "She *seen* all of my bad habits and still loves me."
Correct: "She *has seen* all of my bad habits and now she wants a divorce."
Also correct – using saw (don't use *has, had,* or *have* with *saw*): "She *saw* my bad habit and told me to never let it happen again."

Example 3 – using *had*:

Wrong: "They *seen* the movie together, but he didn't remember it because he spent the entire time on his phone."
Correct: "They *had seen* the movie together, but he didn't remember it because he spent the entire time on his phone."
Also correct – using saw (don't use *has, had* or *have* with *saw*): "He *saw* her walk out on him and just kept looking at his phone."

This issue is not difficult to fix... just put down your phone and watch the movie. ;-)

And now that you better understand the use of *seen* vs. *saw*, you're well on your way to sounding 99% smarter.

I hope you *have seen* the light!

I Have a Great Idea*r*! (Intrusive *Arrrs* are for Pirates!)

I've never seen it spelled this way, but so many people say it. "This way," for those who don't recognize the problem in this chapter's title, is adding an *r* sound to the end of *idea*.

THERE'S NO *R* IN IDEA! People typically pronounce *idea* with an *r* on the end when the word following it starts with a vowel sound. There is NEVER an *r* in the word *idea*. Never. Ever. Not in how it's written or pronounced.

Example – wrong: "I have a great *idear* about how to convince people that the Earth isn't flat!" (Never mind… you can't. Just walk away. Some people aren't worth arguing with. Conspiracy theorists are committed to ignorance disguised as enlightenment.)

Okay, back to the topic at hand.

Unfortunately, the word *idea* isn't the only word where this happens. In the English language there are many words people mispronounce by adding an *r* to the end. It's a real thing, and it even has a name. It's called the "Intrusive R." Most people don't even realize they're saying it, but they *arrr*! It happens when the word following it begins with a vowel sound. Do you remember "vowel sounds" from previous chapters?

Here are more words where people add an Intrusive R:

Pasta: "Anthony heard it would make for a creative picture so he threw the *pastar* against the wall, but the alphabets fell to the floor before he could read what is said."

Media: "The *mediar* asked the politician a question about his opponent and he talked about himself for 10 minutes and no one was surprised!"

Criteria: "What are the *criteriar* applied to deciding who gets a table at this restaurant?" LeBron said as he slipped the maître d' a $100 bill.

Law: "He thought he could beat the *lawr* of gravity by sucking in his gut, but the pictures showed otherwise."

Saw: "He *sawr* an opportunity to impress her with his sarcastic humor, but instead of laughing she punched him in the face and it was *she* who left *him* in stitches."

There are also a number of U.S. State names where the Intrusive R is used:

California: "I love *Californiar* avocados, especially the ones from Mexico," said the valley girl.

Virginia: "*Virginiar* is for lovers..." of "broilers", which are 5 to 12-week-old chickens and the state's top agricultural product. It's a fact. ;-(

Georgia: "I went to *Georgiar* after I heard they have a lot of penis farms there," said Stormy, the blonde woman.

Florida: "The *Floridar* alligators are known for evading golf carts driven by drunken golfers." (As reported by the Mar-a-Lago Times.)

There are more, so just be aware and I'm sure you'll find them. If you catch yourself using the Intrusive R, remember: Save the *arrr* for the pirates!

Dave Bastien

Literally!

The word *literally* has undergone a bizarre transformation. This word that means "actually" or "without exaggeration" is being used by many people... to *exaggerate*!

For instance, someone might say, "I ate so much that I'm *literally* going to explode!" Really, is that "actually" going to happen? Is that statement "without exaggeration?"

Using *literally* to mean its opposite is like saying Republican presidents have been fiscally conservative, even though every Republican president in my lifetime has blown out the federal deficit. And I voted for several of them. I *literally* did!

Example 1: "I *literally* took a dump that overflowed the toilet!" This is *literally* impossible, which means it's an incorrect use of the word, and also an exaggeration of the turd.

Example 2: "She *literally* had an orgasm when she tasted their chicken parmesan." While I'll admit that the Olive Garden restaurant's chicken parmesan is delicious, it's a stretch to say that consuming it *literally* initiated an orgasm.

I think you get the message here... use *literally* literally.

If you're speaking figuratively, just don't say "literally" and we'll surely all get the metaphorical reference.

Infamous vs. *famous*

Similarly, *infamous* is also often misused. People use it to mean someone or something is exceptionally *famous* – in a good way – when it means to have an exceptionally bad reputation.

You should read this entire book so you don't become *infamous* for your poor use of the English language!

Then vs. Than

This may sound like a broken record, but *then* vs. *than* is another simple, careless mistake. Also, like so many others, it's simple to fix. Here's how: read their f*cking definitions! Yes, they sound alike, but way too many people don't understand that they're two separate words. If you haven't gotten the hint yet, I'll say it clearly: *Use. A. Dictionary.* Be curious, look 'em up!

Using *then*:

Definition: Refers to *time* or *consequence*.

> **Example 1 – referring to time:** She said, "I'll take the shot of tequila first, *then* I'll suck on the lime." In this example, *then* refers to time, in that one happens *after* the other.

> **Example 2 – referring to consequence:** She said, "If I drink too much tequila, *then* my clothes will fall off." This is an example of *then* referring to consequence, in that one happens *because* of the other.

Using *than*:

Definition: Refers to a *comparison*, a *difference* between things.

> **Example 1:** "I like tequila better *than* whiskey, because I'm just that kind of girl." This statement refers to a comparison.

> **Example 2:** "Margaritas with salt are better *than* margaritas without salt, unless, of course, you have no salt... *then* they're just as good." In this example, *than* refers to a comparison, and *then* refers to a consequence.

See? Using *then* vs. *than* is easier *than* you thought... once you look 'em up!

Dave Bastien

Let's Talk Punctuation

GRAMMAR NERD ALERT: This is by far the longest and one of the more grammar-nerdish chapters. I've done my best to translate the rules to simplify the use of punctuation. There are lots of examples, too. So please have a little patience and you'll come out on the other side of this one 99% smarter! Let's begin...

When I say, "Let's talk punctuation," I also mean the lack thereof. Missing punctuation is only visible (or invisible!) in writing (duh!), and these days it happens most commonly on social media, in text messages, and in email.

Sure, there are people who over-punctuate, too, and we'll get to that. But one of my biggest pet peeves is when people who post on social media use no punctuation at all – no matter how long the post is!

Here's an example WITHOUT punctuation:

Mike does it Sarah does it too I get frustrated when I see posts without any punctuation I wish I had a nickel for every missing comma or period how can people not see it their writing doesn't make any sense without punctuation they must be idiots

Here's the example WITH punctuation:

Mike does it. Sarah does it, too. I get frustrated when I see posts without any punctuation. I wish I had a nickel for every missing comma or period! How can people not see it?! Their writing doesn't make any sense without punctuation. They must be idiots!

Punctuation breaks up what you say into groups of words that are easier to understand. It controls the flow and inflection, and it creates pauses that separate sentences into more meaningful and structured parts. *If you want people to understand what you're trying to say, you have to use punctuation.* Included in this chapter are just the basic forms... those that will make you 99% smarter!

About the rules

There are a shitload of punctuation rules, and I won't include them all here. You'd get overwhelmed with grammar-nerd speak and stop reading this book, which means you'd never *Smarten the F*ck Up!* So, if you really want to master the use of punctuation, master this chapter first, then look up more details over a beer or two. A glass of wine would work, too. Preferably red, since punctuation is read. (There's a homophone for ya!) ;-)

When you look up punctuation rules, you'll find some where you say "f*ck this" because they just make your head explode, but then there are others where you'll actually learn something. Don't give up! You may have to read some over and over before they make sense. Remember... it's about the 99%.

HERE'S A TIP FOR READING GRAMMAR RULES: If a rule makes your head explode, *focus on the examples* and you'll likely learn more than from reading the rule itself. Rules are typically loaded with grammar-speak, but the examples are usually simple and clear.

Let's get started with using punctuation!

Periods... we'll begin with the end.

First, the simplest one: a *period*. Yes, that single little dot. After you've written a complete thought, end it with a period. It means *stop*. Just put it where you would stop to take a breath when you're talking. A period represents the end of a sentence.

(As I write this, I'm reminded of all my friends who can talk up a storm and never take a breath. They seem to be able to breathe through their nose and talk at the same time. It may be alcohol that gives them this superpower, but sometimes you've got tell them to put a cork in it. They're probably the ones who don't know about periods, too!)

When you put a period at the end of a sentence, remember... *it's not preceded by a space!* I can't understand how someone could ever get through grammar school thinking that a space goes before a period, but I see it often on social media. Never add a space before punctuation that ends a sentence, such as a period, exclamation point, or a question mark.

Some people even use periods to emphasize each word. That's just a style thing, but it's... Not. My. Style.

What's a comma? It's the pause that refreshes!

Commas are used to separate words, phrases, and clauses, and to create a logical pause in a sentence. Sure, there are rules, but in general they should be used where you would naturally have a soft pause to be clearly understood when reading or speaking. Putting commas in all the right places is challenging for most of us. If I had to choose, my preference would be to see people err on the side of using a few too many, rather than omitting them completely.

Here are a few examples where commas matter:

Example 1: "Let's eat Grampa Dave!" vs. "Let's eat, Grampa Dave!"

Example 2: "Most of the time travelers worry about their luggage." vs. "Most of the time, travelers worry about their luggage."

Example 3: "My dog goes outside to eat poop and bark." vs. "My dog goes outside to eat, poop, and bark."

Some simple rules for using commas.

Don't get stuck on the grammar-speak in the descriptions below. It's all explained in simple terms for each example:

1. After an introductory clause: An introductory clause simply introduces the main topic of the sentence.

> **Here's a simple example:** "After she checked his bank account balance, she went on a shopping spree." In this example, "After she checked his bank account balance" is the *introductory clause,* meaning it introduces the main topic of the sentence, "she went on a shopping spree." Pretty simple, huh?

2. Between two independent clauses: An independent clause is one that can stand on its own as a complete sentence. In addition to using a comma, two independent clauses are joined by a conjunction (and, but, then, so, because, etc.)

> **Here's a simple example:** "He went to the baseball game, then he went out for beers with the guys." In this example, "He went to the baseball game" works fine as a stand-alone sentence, and "he went out for beers with the guys" also works fine as a stand-alone sentence. They're two *independent clauses* combined into a single sentence, so you separate them with a comma – and the appropriate conjunction (and, but, then, so, because, etc). This is a piece-of-cake rule!

3. Between items in a series or list: This is one of the simpler uses of commas. Here are a couple of examples:

Example 1: "Mark was tasked with starting the bonfire, so he watched several YouTube videos and then bought firewood, kindling, paper, matches, and gasoline."

Example 2 – using items in a series that are more than one word: "When Sarah goes home to visit her parents, she wants to go candlepin bowling, visit her favorite hangout by the river, have dinner with her ex-boyfriend, and show him her new engagement ring."

4. To separate a nonrestrictive clause: I know, I know… you're saying, "What the f*ck is a nonrestrictive clause?" It's really very simple: it's one that's not essential to the meaning of the sentence. Some people call it a "nonessential clause."

Example: "Susan, who likes to garden, cleared half an acre of brush with her bare hands to plant sunflowers." The clause "who likes to garden" is considered *nonrestrictive* because it's not essential to the meaning of the sentence, so it's separated from the rest using commas. It's really not that difficult, right? (This is a true story about my wife.)

5. To separate an appositive: This is another WTF?! Don't worry. An *appositive* is just the grammar nerd term for a noun or noun phrase that renames (or specifies) a nearby noun. I know, you're still saying "WTF?!" Here's a simple example:

Example: "Mr. Munster, the undertaker, drove his kids around the neighborhood in a hearse every Halloween." The phrase "the undertaker" renames "Mr. Munster", so it's an *appositive*. I don't make up the rules, folks; I'm just trying to simplify them through examples.

6. To indicate direct address: When you name the person to whom you're speaking, it's called a direct address. It can be anywhere in the sentence. Here's an example:

Example: "Mom, I don't want to go to school today!" Or this: "Stop being an asshole and correcting everything I say, Dave." When you directly address someone by name or title, use a comma to set off their name or title.

7. To set off a direct quotation: This one is pretty easy, too.

Example: "Mary said, 'This chapter on punctuation is too f*cking long!'" The comma after the word *said* sets off her direct quotation.

8. With dates, addresses, titles, and numbers:

Example with dates: "On February 29th, 2020, Madi was the first baby born on leap day!"

Example with addresses: The elements of an address are separated by commas, except for the zip code: "Please send your payment via cash or check to Maggie Magpie, 777 Oak Tree Road, Capital City, New York 99999."

Example with titles: When a title follows a person's name, separate the title with a pair of commas. Here's an example: "Mr. Digger, the Grave Cemetery General Manager, always joked that his cemetery was so popular people were dying to get in."

Example with numbers: Use commas to separate numbers into groups of three, starting from the right. For example: "Depending on whom you ask, the number of people who attended the political rally was somewhere between 350 and 3,500,000."

Apostrophes

Apostrophes matter! Which restaurant would you rather visit?

This one: "The hostess went into the waiting room and called the guests names."

Or this one: "The hostess went into the waiting room and called the guests' names."

A well-placed apostrophe is also the difference between "knowing your shit" and "knowing you're shit." In this case, it's used to create the contraction of "you are." As we've seen in other chapters, apostrophes are used in contractions to replace the missing letters when words are combined.

They're also used to indicate a missing letter when writing out an informal pronunciation of a word: "I got paid nothin' for my time." Although it's not a formal use of an apostrophe, at least it does somethin' to help you understand the pronunciation.

To indicate possession: When indicating possession – who the owner is – the 99% rule is this: if the word doesn't end in *s*, add *'s*. If the word ends in *s*, just add an *apostrophe*. It's a very simple rule.

> **Example 1** – when it's something that only one dog possesses: "The *dog's* fart cleared the room."

This is how it's written when only one dog does it, although I can usually tell which one it was by the look on their face. (The smile gives it away!)

Example 2 – when it's something that belongs to all of the dogs: "The *dogs'* barks announced the arrival of the Hawaiian Chipotle pizza with anchovies."

In general, if the word already ends with the letter *s*, just add an *apostrophe* to make it possessive. (FYI… Hawaiian Chipotle pizza with anchovies is the only kind the dogs won't steal from the table. Maybe any pizza with anchovies would work, though.)

And while we're on the topic of using *'s* for possession, next time you wish someone a Happy (whatever) Day remember, use *'s* only for Mother's Day, Father's Day, Valentine's Day, and New Year's Day, because they are possessive (meaning it's their day). Also, it's just Happy New Year, not Happy New Year's or Years. The word "Veterans" in Veterans Day is plural, meaning we celebrate all veterans, so there's no *apostophe* on that, either.

Important note: Possession using pronouns is different. See the chapter "WTF is a Possessive Pronoun?"

Don't make this common mistake!

While we're on the topic of apostrophes, here's a common mistake people make regarding when an *'s* should *not* be used.

Never use *'s* to make a noun plural! To do that (that is, to indicate more than one), simply add an *s*. No apostrophe… just an *s*. This covers 99% of all nouns.

Example – wrong: "My *dog's* love to sniff the baby's bum."

Example – correct: "My *dogs* love to sniff the baby's bum."

I'll repeat: Never use *'s* to make a noun plural! (And isn't it great that I trained my dogs to let me know when it's time for a diaper change? I can only hope one of them lives long enough to help me out when I'm older!)

Question marks

Next up, the question mark. Its use is straightforward because it punctuates a question. Duh! Can you understand that? (See what I did there?)

Some people even use three for emphasis. Have you ever seen that??? Although it's not grammatically correct, people use multiple question marks to express doubt, disbelief, confusion, or excitement.

For example, when you get an email from Prince Sahara in the Middle East saying he's decided to give away his fortune and needs your bank account information to make a $1,000,000 deposit, you might respond with "Really???" to express your doubt, disbelief, confusion, or excitement... depending on how gullible you are.

A question mark is one of the simplest forms of punctuation. And for God's sake, why would anyone ever put a space before a question mark ? Don't ever do this! It's just wrong.

Exclamation points

Exclamation points are frequently overused. They're used to express things like excitement, surprise, emphasis, or shouting.

Example: You could say, "He finally put his dirty dishes in the dishwasher!" Or you could use the social media edition and say, "He finally put his dirty dishes in the dishwasher!!!" You decide... does using three mean more than one?

If you feel like putting three after your sentence to exaggerate your point, go ahead!!! Just promise you'll never use more than three. There's never a need for a whole line of them!!!!!!!!!!!!!!!!!!!!!!!!!!!!

Also, as a general guideline, you should avoid using them in consecutive sentences or more than once in a paragraph.

Interrobangs

The name *interrobang* comes from the formal name for the question mark, which is an *interrogation point,* and the informal name typesetters have for an exclamation point, which is a *bang.* It's the newest punctuation mark and was first introduced in 1962 by Martin K. Speckter, an American advertising executive.

The interrobang, which I used a few pages back ("WTF?!"), combines a question mark and an exclamation point. It's intended to invoke a question – typically a rhetorical one – with emphasis, excitement, or disbelief.

This informal punctuation mark is becoming popular, especially on social media. There's even a formal character for it, which is an exclamation point superimposed on a question mark – ‽ – but you won't find it on your keyboard. Most people use a combination of question marks and exclamation points: ?!, !?, ?!? or !?! And to those who feel a need to use longer combinations of both, all I can say is, "Are you kidding me?!?!?!?!"

Hyphens and dashes

Hyphens are used to glue words together. When two or more words function as one to form a single, more specific meaning, they should be hyphenated. And hyphens have no spaces on either side, because, if they did, the word-glue wouldn't hold. ;-)

There are also instances where you're using two or more words in combination to express a specific thought, and, in your judgment, a hyphen would help convey your meaning with more clarity. That's a perfectly acceptable justification for use. Here are some of the rules:

Writer's judgment: "She was clearing a spot in the backyard for her garden and became a *bush-lopping* maniac!"

Conveying ages: "Noah's *60-year-old* grandma was very proud when her *4-year-old* grandson recited the planet names by heart." (It's easier now than when we were kids. We had to remember 9 of them!)

Spelled out fractions: "*Two-thirds* of those who read this book will feel embarrassed about a stupid mistake they've been making for *one-half* of their life."

For clarity:

    Example 1: "I saw a *man eating* fish" vs. "I saw a *man-eating* fish."

    Example 2: "I'll give you *twenty-five* dollar bills" vs. "I'll give you twenty *five-dollar* bills." Which would you rather have?

    Example 3: "Twenty *four-hour* shifts" vs. "*Twenty-four* hour shifts" vs. "*Twenty-four-hour* shifts."

When on a rant: "The *self-declared* genius politician went on a *lie-infested* response to a question from the press, focusing on a totally *off-topic* issue because he was *butt-hurt*."

Dashes

I know what you're thinking… "WTF? A dash is different from a hyphen?" You're confused because you thought a hyphen and a dash were the same thing, and there's only one character for it on your keyboard.

To make it even more confusing, there are two types of dashes: the *en dash*, which is about the width of the capital letter N, and the *em dash*, which is about the width of the capital letter M. They each have specific uses.

The *en dash* is used with numbers, spans or estimates of time, distance, or other quantities:

NOTE: The *en dash* is not used when a span or range is introduced with *from* or *between*. With *from*, use *to*. With *between*, use *and*.

"It was scheduled to last *from* 2:00 *to* 3:30 p.m. and they expected 100–150 people, but *between* 400 *and* 500 showed up to watch them catapult pumpkins carved in his image into a brick wall!"

In informal writing, such as on social media, lots of people use hyphens instead of an *en dash*, and that's perfectly fine to convey the correct meaning, especially since the character isn't readily available on a standard keyboard. If you're writing a resume, or anything else of importance, be sure to get it right.

The *em dash* is very versatile and a bit artistic for punctuation. It's typically used to indicate a pause and can replace a pair of commas, a colon, or parentheses.

An *em dash*—the extra-long dash—is used to draw attention to information, as I did here, or it can be used to call attention to something at the end of a sentence—like this. It usually doesn't have spaces on either side. It's also acceptable to use an *en dash* with spaces on either side for the same purpose, as I've done in this book.

More rules: Not surprisingly, there are more rules on hyphens and dashes, but those listed here will certainly cover the 99%. If you're hyphen-ventilating about this form of punctuation, feel free to look 'em up, although you'll likely never use them.

There are 14 types of punctuation, but these are the most commonly used. If this chapter inspires you to dig a bit deeper, a quick search will provide hours – if not days – of head-spinning, mind-boggling grammar speak. Again, focus on the examples to learn more!

Punctuation on Your Phone

Smartphone the F*ck Up!

Now, after that last chapter, we're going to eliminate all excuses for not using punctuation.

Many people exclusively use their smartphone to communicate these days, and lots of them say they don't use punctuation because they use speech-to-text or talk-to-text. Well, guess what? Your phone is smarter than you think. It knows punctuation!

Did you know you can say "comma" or "period" – or even "ellipsis" – and your phone will insert it for you? How cool is that?! Now that you know this little trick there are no more excuses for f*cking up punctuation in a text, post, or email. I know you have your phone in front of you right now, so go ahead and try it – I'll wait...

See? Wasn't that awesome?

And here's another trick: the long-press. If you long-press on the "hyphen" key, it brings up a visual menu of a hyphen, an en dash and an em dash. How cool is that?! A long-press on the period will let you select an ellipsis. Try all the keys to explore the possibilities. And if your smartphone keyboard doesn't do all that you want it to, you can even download a new keyboard! Just search for one in your app store.

These simple tricks work with all punctuation marks, so you really have no excuse for talk-texting things that make you sound stupid.

So... get out your phone and *Smartphone the F*ck Up!*

Five Words Used by Funkwumple Rugbuggers!

Reminder... the bold word is (still) the correct one.

1. Ungyion vs. **Onion:** There's no *g* in *onion.* Some people who don't like them might say there is... as in, *g* for gross. Personally, I love them, especially fried in butter and dropped on a steak and cheese sub... or a hoagie, hero, grinder, blimp, zeppelin, torpedo, spuckie, or bomber – depending on where you're from. But no matter what you call the sandwich, there's only one way to pronounce *onion.*

2. Pitcher vs. **Picture** – I'm sure everyone knows the difference between these two. This is just an example of people not taking the time to pronounce it correctly. Don't be a lazy dictioner!

3. On Accident vs. **By Accident:** The proper phrase is *by accident.* Saying "on accident" makes you sound like a 3-year-old who hasn't learned it yet... "I peed my pants on accident." Yes, you'll find people who say it's acceptable; probably the same ones who say farting in public is acceptable. But I have to be a Negative Nike here and say, "Just *don't* do it!" And don't use "on accident" either!

4. Probally or prolly vs. **Probably:** If you say *probally* or *prolly* you might as well just walk around town with a dunce cap on, because that's what people will think of you the second the word leaves your lips. It's *probably.*

5. Libary vs. **Library:** If you think the place where they keep all the books is called a libary, then you've probably never been to one. But I have good news for you... it's not too late. You can get a library card for free and read all the books you want... even this one!

Dave Bastien

Who vs. Whom

Let me start by saying that most of us will still get this one wrong when speaking. We just won't think fast enough as the words are being flicked from our habit-formed tongues. But when writing, we can all apply the following rule and get it 100% right!

As with much of this book, these basic rules will make you 99% smarter when using *who* vs. *whom*. As usual, there are exceptions that will leave you cross-eyed, so feel free to look 'em up (but you might end up with an appointment to see your ophthalmologist).

<u>The basic rule</u> (this one is a bit grammar-nerdish): *Who* is a *subject* pronoun, and *whom* is an *object* pronoun.

Before you get your brain get twisted into a pretzel, read on a bit further.

Who **is used to refer to the *subject* of a sentence: <u>the one doing something</u>.**

> **Example:** "*Who* the f*ck put the mouse trap in my slippers?" In this case my wife is the *who*. She's the one doing something, so *who* is the correct word. It's the *subject* pronoun. (She still laughs about it all these years later, but my revenge is patient.)

Whom **is used to refer to the *object* of a sentence: <u>the one having something done to it</u>.**

> **Example:** After the trap was tripped, I said – after several choice expletives – "The mouse trap was meant for *whom*?" In this case I'm the *object* of my wife's prank, so *whom* is the correct word. It's the *object* pronoun.

Like I said at the beginning of this chapter, most of us will still get this one wrong when speaking, but here's a little trick to getting it right in writing:

The trick... when it's used in a question:

- If you can answer the question with *he* or *she*, use *who*.
- If you can answer the question with *him* or *her*, use *whom*.

Example – using *who*: "*Who* left a single sheet of toilet paper on the roll knowing that I have diarrhea?" The answer is *he did*, because *he* can play a prank too! And *him did* just doesn't sound right. So, in this case *who* is the correct word.

Example – using *whom*: "Against *whom* was she planning her next prank, the one where the cover comes off the ketchup?" The answer is *against him*, because he deserves it and it's her turn. And "She's planning the prank against *he*" just doesn't sound right. So, in this case *whom* is the correct word.

Like I said, you're likely to continue making this mistake for a while. It takes more thinking and awareness than most of the other things in this book, but you'll get there... and maybe someday I will, too!

In the meantime, watch out for those people who use the word *whom* to sound smarter than you. Some folks use it to make themselves feel grammatically superior, but you can just smile and let them have their way because, as you read this book, you're almost certain to find an opportunity to take them down a notch or two and show them who is truly grammatically superior. Read on, so you'll be prepared for the pretentious assholes!

Who vs. That

The 99% rule on using *who* vs. *that* is simple:

The rule: When referring to a human being or an animal with a name, say *who*, and when referring to an object, say *that*.

Those who make up these rules probably included the "animal with a name" caveat because most of us anthropomorphize (attribute human qualities to) our pets. We give them more nicknames than we do most of our loved ones!

This rule is a bit more flexible than others. For instance, it's okay to sometimes use *that* when referring to people, but it's never okay to use *who* when referring to objects.

Using *Who*:

Example 1: "The woman *who* called me an asshole must not have known that I already knew that." (Otherwise, why would she tell me?) In this case *who* is correct because it refers to a woman – a human being (although not a very nice one).

Example 2: "My dog, Taylor, *who* sits under the table at dinner, is better at cleaning plates than my dishwasher!" (Yes, he's even better than my super-expensive new Kenmore with the ultra-quiet SmartWash™ cycle!) In this case *who* is correct because it refers to "an animal with a name," my awesome dog, Taylor.

Using *That*:

Example 1: "The cab *that* picked me up was not the one I called, so I ended up at the airport instead of the grocery store." (If I hadn't spent the entire trip staring at my phone, I would've known we were going to the wrong place!) In this case *that* is correct because it refers to the cab – an object.

Example 2: "I don't know if it's because my timing was impeccable or if it was the skill of the bird *that* flew over my head as I looked up, but thank God I was wearing sunglasses!" (Sometimes you just can't make shit up that's better than reality.) In this case *that* is correct because it refers to the bird – an object.

There is one important exception to the *who* vs. *that* rule: owls never have to use the word *that*. ;-)

That vs. Which

The words *that* and *which* are each used to introduce a clause in a sentence. *A clause is simply a group of words that are part of a sentence.*

To use *that* vs. *which*, all you need to understand about clauses is the difference between restrictive and nonrestrictive ones... and it's way easier than you think! (Okay... you're saying, "He said there'd be no grammar-nerd language, but restrictive vs. nonrestrictive clauses is f*cking killin' me!" You can handle this... I promise. Just read on.)

Restrictive clauses

Some clauses are integral to the meaning of the sentence. They're called *restrictive* because they restrict the meaning of the sentence in a specific way. Restrictive clauses are introduced in the sentence by the word *that*. (Examples are below.)

Nonrestrictive clauses

Some clauses, if removed, don't significantly change the meaning of the sentence. Want to guess what they're called? *Nonrestrictive.* Nonrestrictive clauses are introduced in the sentence by the word *which*. (You might remember nonrestrictive clauses from the chapter on punctuation, the section on commas. Some people also call them *nonessential* clauses.) (Examples are below.)

Pretty straightforward, huh? Okay, maybe not yet, but here are examples:

Example 1 – a restrictive clause using *that*: "My home *that has five bathrooms* is used as the party house for my bowling team."

151

The clause "that has five bathrooms" is a *restrictive clause* because it specifies which home I'm referring to. It conveys that I have other homes, but it's the one with five bathrooms that's used as the party house. (Bathrooms are important to a party house, unless it also has a yard with a lot of trees.) Because the clause is integral to the meaning of the sentence, the correct word to use is *that*, and it's not set off by commas.

> **Example 2 – a nonrestrictive clause using *which*:** "My home, *which has five bathrooms*, is used as the party house for my bowling team."

This example presents the fact that my home has five bathrooms as a descriptive detail. (This could also be seen as bragging.) ;-). It doesn't, like the previous example, convey that I have other homes. The information is interesting, but leaving it out wouldn't change the meaning of the sentence. Therefore, it's a *nonrestrictive* clause, introduced by *which* and set off by commas.

Here are more examples:

> **Example 3 – using *that*:** "He finally cut up the tree *that fell on his house* during the thunderstorm."

The clause "that fell on his house" restricts which tree he cut up. Of the several possible candidates, this example makes it clear that it's the tree that fell on his house during the thunderstorm that was cut up, so it's a *restrictive clause.* (And saying *finally* also makes it clear that he's a lazy SOB and a procrastinator.)

> **Example 4 – using *which*:** "He finally cut up the tree, which fell on his house, during the thunderstorm."

When you remove the clause "which fell on his house" this sentence says that the tree was cut up in the middle of the thunderstorm. It's a *nonrestrictive* clause. This sentence could be written more clearly, because cutting up a tree during a thunderstorm isn't a very smart thing to do, especially if you have an electric chain saw!

Summary: If the information in the clause is essential to the meaning of the sentence, use *that*, and no commas. If it just adds information that's useful but not necessary, use *which*, and don't forget the commas!

And here's an interesting tidbit on using *that* and *which*: when used together they mean "what." For instance, the quote "*That which* doesn't kill you makes you stronger" can also be said as "What doesn't kill you makes you stronger."

This grammar book certainly won't kill you, but it *will* make you stronger!

Dave Bastien

There's vs. There Are

The most common mistake with using *there's* is that people don't understand – or they just ignore – what the contraction represents. *There's* a lot of people who make this mistake. (As I just did here!)

There's **is a contraction for** *there is* **or** *there has.*

Would you ever say, "*There is* a lot of people who make this mistake?" You shouldn't, but that's what you're saying if you use the contraction *there's*. What you should say is, "*There are* a lot of people who make this mistake."

There're is a perfectly acceptable contraction for *there are*, but it's seldom used because it doesn't save any syllables, as contractions are meant to do. Most people just use *there are*.

Here are more examples:

> **Example – incorrect:** "*There's* many intelligent people who don't believe we landed on the moon." Without the contraction, this sentence reads, "*There is* many intelligent people who don't believe we landed on the moon." This is clearly not the way it should be said... for a couple of reasons!

> **Example – correct:** "*There are* many intelligent people who don't believe we landed on the moon." Grammatically, it's now correct, but calling these people intelligent clearly is not.

> **Example – correct – using** *there's* **as a contraction for** *there has*: "*There's* been a lot of interest in crazy conspiracy theories lately."

As illustrated in the examples above, *there are* many people for whom facts have become opinions and proven science has become fiction. They're a clear example of what causes people to say stupid things that this book can't fix!

Here's vs. here are

Here's vs. *here are* is the same problem. *Here's* is a contraction for *here is*, but people constantly use it in place of *here are*. Even Amazon's Alexa gets this one wrong! Try this: say, "Alexa... give me a recipe for meatballs" (or whatever). She'll respond with, "Okay... for meatballs. *Here's* a few recipes."

Someone from Amazon will probably read this and fix Alexa's mistake before you get around to hearing it. I only mention this example to make a point: even professionals make mistakes. You can find them in just about any book, including this one, I'm sure. So – as with most things in life – don't expect perfection, but I'm confident you can get to 99%!

Here's the bottom line to this chapter: *there's* no reason for you to ever make this mistake again, although *there are* many people who occasionally will... including me!

Lie vs. Lay

I'm including this chapter because a friend recently made a big issue out of my choice of words (I was wrong) because he knew I was writing a book about grammar.

Here's our conversation over a few beers: I said, "When using *lie* vs. *lay*, regardless of which word you use, people will understand what the f*ck you mean... seriously." He responded, "But you're writing this big f*cking book about grammar, and you make mistakes yourself!" I said, "Yes, and I forgive myself for an occasional mistake, and you should forgive yourself, too... even if I don't!" He said, "I get it... the 99% rule, right?" Then we had a toast to *Smarten the F*ck Up,* as he finally grasped the concept.

We all make mistakes. None of us gets it all right, but we can get it right 99% of the time. And that's what I'm focused on helping people do with this book. So forgive yourself for the occasional mistake. You're not alone!

On to the topic of this chapter...

Let's set aside the definition of *lie*, as in, "He told a *lie* every time he opened his mouth." We're focused on *lie* vs. *lay*, which is where people – like me – mess up. If you really want to use *lie* vs. *lay* correctly, here are the details:

Lie means to rest or recline, as in to *lie* down; *to assume a horizontal position.*

> **Example:** At my first massage appointment my wife said, "Just *lie* on the table and shut up." (My wife is a massage therapist and prefers that people not talk during their massage.)

Lay means to put or place something somewhere, and *it requires an object/thing.*

Example: At my second massage appointment she said, "Please *lay* your clothes over the chair, instead of dropping them on the floor like you did last time. You're not at home, you know!"

As you can see from the examples above, using the present tense form of each word isn't very difficult, and these are the ones that will make you 99% smarter. Don't bother looking up the various tenses, because it gets a confusing and will only make you tense. ;-) Here they are, just so you can see what I mean:

Forms of *lie*: lie, lay, have lain, lying

Forms of *lay*: lay, laid, have laid, laying

The only people who really give a shit about the distinction between these words are the true grammar-nerd dickheads... like my friend. You don't have to be one of them and people will still know what you mean!

P.S. *Sit* vs. *set* follows the same rule. You can *sit* wherever and whenever you want, but to *set* something requires an object.

On to more important things!

Dave Bastien

A Lot vs. Alot

I see this mistake *alot!* Or is it *a lot?* This is an easy one to fix!

The rule: *A lot* is always two words. Period. Full stop. End of discussion.

Consider this: Would you ever write *alittle?* Would you ever write *abunch?* Would you ever write *ashit-ton?* (Yes, shit-ton is a word.)

These are rhetorical questions, of course, which should be intuitively obvious to the most casual observer; but no, you would never write any of these as one word.

Allot (a different spelling) is also a word, and it means "to distribute, to share a portion, or give someone a share of something; to allocate or apportion." It's a word that isn't used *a lot,* though.

Just remember that *a lot* is *two syllables* and *two words.* As in, "The smart writer knows to always allot a space between the words *a* and *lot.*" You should, too!

And while we're on the subject, here are a couple of similar common mistakes. I'm sure there are more, but my point in presenting these is: if you don't know, look it up!

No one: *No one* is always two words. *No one* should ever say *noone.*

Alright: As one word, *alright* means okay. As two words, it means everything that you're referring to is correct, as in, the answers are *all right.*

Cannot: *Cannot* is always one word and *can't* is the contraction. The only time *can not* is written as two words is when the word *can* comes before a phrase that starts with *not,* as in: "Ignoring science *can not* only be deadly, it can also expose one's inherent stupidity!"

Five More Words Used by Lumpheaded Dingbats

Reminder... the bold word is the correct one!

Adding syllables to words is an especially obnoxious habit. These are some of the most common examples:

1. Realator vs. **Realtor:** Waaay too many people add a syllable to this word. One who sells real estate is a *real-tor* – just two syllables. *Realtors* are called many things by their clients, but *real-a-tor* shouldn't be one of them!

2. Athelete vs. **Athlete:** There are just two syllables in this word, too: ath-lete. It's not ath-e-lete. Jocks might want to think that their *ath* is *e-lete*, but the smart kids know better!

3. Triathalon vs. **Triathlon:** This one has a clue right in the f*cking word itself: tri. The prefix *tri* means three. The word has three syllables: it's *tri-ath-lon*, not *tri-ath-a-lon*.

4. Irregardless vs. **Regardless:** Irregardless isn't a real word, although this mistake has become so common that some dictionaries have added it – mainly to point out that it's the incorrect use of *regardless*. It has a negative prefix, *ir-*, and a negative suffix, *-less*, which makes irregardless mean "not without regard", which is the opposite of regardless. So, drop the double negative and don't not use the correct form of the word, which is *regardless*.

5. Mischievious vs. **Mischievous:** This mispronounced word adds a syllable that's a single letter – *i*. There's no *i-o-u* in *mischievous*, unless you're being *mischievous* and you prank someone... then you should expect an i-o-u. (I know... my sense of humor can be difficult to understand sometimes.)

Personal
vs.
Personally

Saying "Don't take it personal" instead of "Don't take it personally" is another very common mistake.

I could get into a full grammar-nerd discussion about adverbs and adjectives and how they relate to verbs and nouns, but I know for many of you – and sometimes for me, too – that's somewhat of a foreign language, so I'll call this one "grammar nerd lite." If you want more detail you can look it up, but meanwhile, I'll get right to the point:

<u>The rule</u>: Anytime you tell someone *"Don't take it personal"*, you're saying it wrong. You should be saying *"Don't take it personally."* This covers 99% of the uses where people get it wrong.

There are lots of other instances where everyone uses these words correctly, but this specific phrase is the one that gets f*cked up all the time.

Here's just a little more for those who want to know. The word *personal* is an adjective, which is a word that describes a noun. For instance:

> **Example – correct – using *personal*:** "He took his *personal* jet to pick her up for their first date." In this sentence, the adjective, *personal,* describes the noun, *jet*, which belongs to him. (Maybe it's just a lease, who the f*ck really knows. She was impressed, either way.)

The word *personally* is an adverb, which is a word that modifies a verb. "Modifies" means to restrict or limit, or in some way define the verb. Here's an example using a different adverb:

Example: "My dog barks *constantly*." The use of the verb, *barks*, is defined by the adverb *constantly*. It adds definition to the verb, hence, it's an adverb!

Here's an example using both words, *personal* and *personally*:

Example – correct – using both words: My friend said to me, "My *personal* opinion is that you're a bigger asshole than you think you are, but don't take it *personally*." (He may be right, so I'll take it objectively.) The adjective, *personal*, describes the noun, *opinion*, and the adverb, *personally*, describes the verb, *take*.

If I had a dollar for every time I've heard someone use the word *personal* when they should use *personally*, I wouldn't be trying to sell this book. But since I am, maybe you know someone who could use a *personal* copy that I could *personally* sign? ;-)

Take it for Granted vs. Take it for Granite

Sorry, but there's no sugar-coating this one.

Granite is a f*cking rock. That's all it is. If you take something for *granite,* all it means is that you're looking at another type of rock and you mistakenly think it's f*cking granite. You're taking it for *granite.*

When you say "Don't take it for *granite*" you sound like a total idiot. Don't do it! The word you need to use is *granted.*

Taking something for *granted* means not appreciating it as much as you should, treating it without the importance it deserves, or taking it as if you're entitled to it… like it's been *granted* to you.

Got it? Good. If this is the only mistake in this book you end up fixing, you'll still sound much smarter – especially in New Hampshire, whose secondary tag line after "Live Free or Die" is "The Granite State." We don't take our *granite* for *granted*!

Coupon vs. *Cyoupon*

How to pronounce the word *coupon* is something I've heard debated many times, and everyone swears their way is correct.

This situation is the opposite of the silent letter problem. In this case, people *add* the letter *y* after the *c* and pronounce the word as *cyupon*. It could also be spelled phonetically as *quepon*.

This has been the topic of much discussion among those of us who've been told we're a bit annoying with all our grammar and pronunciation rules. (Okay, I've been called much worse than just annoying.) But, instead of pointing out who's wrong and who's right, on this one I can assure the masses who swear by their version that they're both right! Both pronunciations are acceptable.

Try this just for fun:

(Warning: this is how grammar nerds have fun at a party!)

The next time you're at a party, ask people how to pronounce the word *coupon*. (*Note: for full enjoyment of the ensuing discussion, wait until everyone has had a few beers... they'll be much more likely to share their enthusiastic opinion with vigorous commitment.*)

One rule is that they can't look it up on their phone first – it must be *their opinion*. Then you can just sit back and have a beer while you enjoy the contentious debate until you've had enough entertainment.

After you've gotten everyone to commit to their pronunciation, type "coupon definition" in a browser on your phone. (Or you can do this in advance and just have the page waiting.) On at least one of the top resulting web pages you'll find pronunciation icons you can tap to show that both versions are correct.

Your friends will be totally impressed, and you can tell them that they, too, can *Smarten the F*ck Up,* and then suggest they get a copy of this book. (I really appreciate the referrals!)

So, next time you go to the checkout at the grocery store, feel free to proudly exclaim, "I have a coupon" with confidence... no matter how you say it! No more mumbling it out of fear of pronouncing it wrong.

P.S. Here's a bonus: you can do the same thing with the words *interesting* and *comfortable.*

Interesting:

Some people pronounce it with four syllables, as in: in-te-rest-ing. Others pronounce it with three syllables, as in: in-trest-ing. Both are considered correct.

Comfortable:

This word is also pronounced with four syllables, as in: comf-or-ta-ble. And it's okay to pronounce it with three syllables, too, as in: comf-ta-ble.

Go ahead... be the life of the party!

Dave Bastien

There's No Backslash in a Website Address!

This is one I hear in radio and TV ads all the time. The announcer will say "Visit blah, blah, blah, *backslash*, blah, blah, blah for more information."

**This is a backslash: **

This is a slash (also called a forward slash): /

If you use a backslash in a website address, you'll never get anywhere. Website addresses (called URLs or Universal Resource Locators) *never* contain a backslash!

I'm surprised there's not more backlash about this one.

First of All, Second of All, Third of All, etc.

First of all, second of all, third of all...

We've all heard people use these phrases to introduce a series of talking points, but saying it this way always seems so awkward. The good news is, there are better options.

Let's start by saying, stay away from using *of all,* at all!

My first experience with this as a problem happened years ago when I used it in a presentation with some co-workers. When I got to "fourth of all", one of them said, "What the f*ck does *of all* mean, anyway? And just how many is *all?*"

It's funny how we get stuck on doing things a certain way until someone jolts us out of it. I had never really thought about this, so I looked it up. Needless to say, I changed how I do presentations and I hope this saves you from having a similar experience.

The best way to introduce a set of talking points is also the simplest:

Option 1:

- "First: Blah, blah, blah..."
- "Second: Blah, blah, blah..."
- "Third: Blah, blah, blah..."

If you really want to emphasize the importance of the first point, saying *"First of all..."* is perfectly fine. Then continue stating your points using *second, third,* etc.

And when you get to the last one, you could say, "And the fourth *and final* point is blah, blah, blah..." or even just "And *finally*, blah, blah, blah..."

Option 2:

Here's another – although less preferred – option to using *of all*:

- "First: Blah, blah, blah…"
- "Secondly: Blah, blah, blah…"
- "Thirdly: Blah, blah, blah…"

Some people say this option sounds pretentious. I agree, but the real problem with this method is that the higher you get (*fourthly, fifthly, sixthly…*) the more awkward it sounds. *Stick to option 1.*

When you're trying to make important points, you want people to focus on those and not become distracted by any awkward intro to them. The first option is the best to accomplish that goal.

Now, remember this… if you have 57 points to make, regardless of which method you use, people will still think it's awkward. And – for my final point – if you see people nodding off during your presentation, you're doing something very, very wrong!

Five Words Used by Yankeestered Wussifers

Reminder... the bold word is the correct one.

1. Windshield Factor vs. **Wind Chill Factor** – The first time I heard someone say "windshield factor", I asked them to repeat what they'd said. Then I asked what it meant, and they said it meant it was cold enough outside to have ice on your windshield. My hysterical laughter made them look it up. After 30 seconds I could see they felt like a fool... without me saying a word. After all, they'd been saying it that way for over 20 years and no one ever questioned them!

2. Loose vs. **Lose** – This one can only happen in writing, but the opposite of win is lose – not *loose*, as many people seem to think. I understand that *choose* rhymes with lose, and not loose, which adds to the confusion, and *chose* doesn't rhyme with *lose*, even though it looks like it should. If you're all tongue-twisted trying to read this and you still don't understand the pronunciation and spelling, here's quick guide: *Loose* – meaning *not tight* – rhymes with *goose*, as in the bird. *Lose* – as in *you didn't win* – rhymes with *fuse*, as in I blow mine when I see this mistake.

3. Ex cetera vs. **Et cetera** (abbreviated as *etc.*) – *Et cetera* means "and so on" or "and so forth" or "this list goes on" and is used in place of stating all of the additional items in the list. When you say e*x cetera* all you're saying is, "I don't know any better." ;-)

4. Spicket vs. **Spigot** – Recently, on a plumber's website, I saw multiple references to *spickets*. I would think that, if anyone should know there's no such thing, it would be a plumber. For those who don't know, a *spigot* is a faucet, and, more typically, an outdoor one. Never hire a plumber who doesn't know what a *spigot* is!

5. Wheelbarrel vs. **Wheelbarrow** – Logically, the term *wheelbarrel* kind of makes sense... after all, you can put stuff in it, and it has a wheel. Sorry, but there's no such thing. A *barrow* is a type of cart,

used to transport things, and a *wheelbarrow* is what it sounds like, a *barrow* balanced on a *wheel* (or sometimes *wheels*), with handles, that you use in your backyard or on a construction site. It's a *wheelbarrow*!

Dave Bastien

Capitalization

Capitalization matters

Capitalization is the difference between helping your Uncle Jack off a donkey and helping your uncle jack off a donkey. (Interestingly, a male donkey is also called a jack.)

The example above demonstrates the importance of using capitalization correctly. When it comes to capitalization, the biggest problem I see is people capitalizing words where it's not warranted.

Here are some common capitalization rules:

1. The first word in a sentence
2. People's names
3. Places – e.g. Niagra Falls, Yellowstone National Park
4. Things with proper names – e.g. Pacific Ocean, North Pole
5. Months and days of the week, holidays, *but not seasons*
6. Titles that appear before a name – e.g. Mayor Papi
7. The word "I"
8. Most words in book titles
9. Acronyms
10. First word of a complete quote
11. Cities, countries, nationalities, and languages
12. Time periods and formal events – e.g. Middle Ages, Olympic Games, World War II

Misusing capitalization:

People often use capitalization when they feel a particular word is Important. That's just not how it Works! It's not a Random Thing to use when you want to. There are Rules for a reason, and that reason is to communicate to your READERS in a way that they Expect. You don't want to DISTRACT them from your message. (Did you notice that I misused capitalization in this paragraph? If not, you're probably someone who commits this *capital* offense.)

This type of seemingly random capitalization actually has a name: "pride capitals." If you really want to emphasize a particular word, it's better to use *italics*, **bold**, or an <u>underline</u>. And don't overdo it… one of them is enough.

To make sure your message is clearly understood, it's important to use best practices of grammar in a manner that's anticipated and expected. When you introduce unexpected practices into your communication, the effectiveness of your message suffers. And no one who puts the effort into writing something they feel is important wants that result. So, don't over-capitalize!

Now, to be clear, I'm not talking about using all caps to indicate you're screaming or pissed off. That's a style thing, and it's totally up to you, YOU F*CKHEAD! ;-)

Here's one last example of the confusion incorrect capitalization can cause. If someone says, "Where does the asshole live?" your answer could either be "In the white house" or "In the White House." One would be true, and the other is just a mistake in capitalization!

Sundee, Mondee, Tuesdee, Etc.

Like I always say... "When it comes to pet peeves, we all have 'em!" This one is a huge pet peeve, so here's my little rant:

How do you pronounce the word *day*? Exactly! Then why the f*ck would you ever say Sundee, Mondee, Tuesdee, Wednesdee, Thursdee, Fridee, or Saturdee?

DAY is NOT pronounced DEE. Would you ever say, "I went to the gym todee"? Of course not, because you never go to the f*cking gym! But even if you did, you'd never say it that way.

End of rant.

If you know someone who says "dee," please share this with them so we can stop this bad habit from getting any worse!

WTF is a Possessive Pronoun?

Hers, Ours, Yours, Theirs, and Its, or WTF is a Possessive Pronoun?

As usual with grammar, the technical term for the part of speech is more intimidating than its actual definition. Let's start by reviewing what a *pronoun* is.

A pronoun is simply a word that takes the place of a noun (a person, place, or thing). Pronouns can save you from having to repeat a noun in a subsequent sentence. Without the pronoun, things can get awkward, as in, "*Suzie* planted a garden. *Suzie's* garden is amazing." Instead of repeating a person's name you could say, "*Suzie* planted a garden. *Her* garden is amazing."

So, WTF is a *Possessive* Pronoun?

Pronouns can be possessive, too. For instance, even though I put a lot of work into helping create it, Suzie is very clear that "The garden is *hers*." (She's possessive, even without pronouns!)

Notice that *hers* – a possessive pronoun – has no *'s*, which is usually used to indicate possession.

This chapter is focused on five *possessive pronouns* people screw up all the time: *hers, ours, yours, theirs,* and *its*. These all end with the letter *s*, but people commonly assume they must end in *'s*. They don't… ever! This is the most common mistake people make when using these words.

<u>The rule</u>: To make pronouns possessive, never use an *'s*.

- Use *hers*, not her's,
- Use *ours*, not our's

- Use *yours*, not your's
- Use *theirs*, not their's
- Use *its*, not it's (see more in the "It's vs. Its" chapter)

Here's an example using possessive pronouns:

Example: "Suzie bought a dozen fresh bagels from Einstein Bros. Bagels. When she came home, she made it clear they were *hers,* not *ours,* so I said, 'I get it, they're *yours.*'"

In this example, *hers* is the pronoun that takes the place of Suzie's name, and it shows possession – the bagels belong to *her. Ours* and *yours* also indicate possession. With possessive pronouns, no *'s* is needed.

(I can't blame her for being possessive about these bagels, though... they're amazing! I can understand why she's not fond of sharing, especially if she has fresh cream cheese... the whipped kind. Sometimes I just take one without asking – the "baker's dozen" one – and I think she notices, but she never says anything. Maybe it's because she loves me, but I think it's because she's in their frequent buyer program.)

The bottom line: *no apostrophe+s ('s)!*

We're so used to the rule that says when you make a noun possessive you add an *'s* that we carry it over to using these pronouns. Don't ever add an *'s* to any of these pronouns, and don't ever hesitate to posess Einstein Bros. Bagels!

Secretaries and Generals

Want to sound like a real lugnut? Say "Secretary of *States*" or "Attorney *Generals*" when you're talking about more than one. So many people f*ck this one up... even national politicians and TV personalities on major cable news networks who focus on politics!

<u>The rule</u>: Pluralize the noun

The nouns here are "secretary" and "attorney," and the additional words in the title just describe what kind of secretary and attorney. Normally, the descriptive word or phrase comes before the noun, but in these – and many other – cases, they come after it. So, the plural is *Secretaries* of State and *Attorneys* General, because we're talking about multiple secretaries and attorneys.

The grammar-nerd name for this is a *compound noun*, which just means the noun is made up of more than one word.

It's the same with *sisters-in-law* (correct) vs. *sister-in-laws* (incorrect), or *brothers-in-law* and even *mothers-in-law*... although having one mother-in-law is more than enough!

There are other types of compound nouns, too, but these are the ones people screw up most often. If you can remember to say them correctly, you'll sound 99% smarter... and that's my goal. If you're curious about others, look 'em up! Just do a search for *compound nouns*, or even *hyphenated compound nouns*.

So remember, when using a compound noun and referencing more than one of whatever it is, *pluralize the noun* – the main thing you're talking about. Do it right so when you go to your next family wedding you can introduce your *sisters-in-law* and not make them regret your spouse's choice!

Coming Down the Pipe?

The only person who should ever be concerned about what's "coming down the pipe" is a septic tank inspector when he sticks his head in your concrete shit collector to check your baffle and someone happens to flush.

The real phrase is "coming down the pike"

Saying "coming down the pipe" is a just another careless, lazy mistake. It takes less than 30 seconds to do a search and find that the correct phrase (officially called an idiom) is *coming down the pike*. (There… I just saved you 30 seconds, you lazy SOB!) ;-)

The idiom *coming down the pike* refers to *coming down the turnpike*, which is like saying "coming down the road." When you talk about what's *coming down the pike,* you're simply referring to something that's coming in the future, or "in the course of events."

If you're presenting at a plumbing convention and you really want to use a pipe metaphor, maybe you could use "coming down the *pipe*" and get away with it. You might also consider using *in the pipeline* to refer to something that's being developed or coming in the future. Or you could just ask your septic tank inspector what "coming down the pipe" means to him. I'm sure you'd get hours of shitty stories!

And while we're talking about misunderstood idioms, here's another common one:

One of the most egregious incorrectly used idioms is the phrase "for all intensive purposes." What the f*ck does that really mean? Think about it. *Nothing*. It's simply a stupid thing to say. If you look up "for all intensive purposes" you'll see the correct phrase is "for all intents and purposes," which means "in every practical sense."

I point out the absurdity of this one in particular because when you understand the true meaning or origin of a phrase, you can see the nonsensical reference you're using and you'll be less likely to ever repeat the mistake and sound like a fool. There's absolutely no practical meaning that even the most creative mind could conjure up to justify using "for all intensive purposes" in place of "for all intents and purposes."

I only included these two examples of misunderstood idioms to make this point: if you don't clearly understand what you're saying, look it up! We all have a personal encyclopedic device (smart phone) at our fingertips so there's no excuse.

Personally, I enjoy looking up the origins of sayings. If you want to see more idioms you've misused to inadvertently make a fool of yourself, do an internet search for "misunderstood idioms." There are lots of them.

Five Words That Make You Sound Stupider Than a Piglicker

Reminder... the bold word is the correct one.

1. Deep-seeded vs. **Deep-seated** – As I've pointed out many times, most of these mistakes are made by those who don't read very much. A farmer might use the phrase *deep-seeded* to describe a type of crop planting, but those who have good grammar have a *deep-seated* tradition of reading.

2. "Can you repeat that again?" vs. **"Can you repeat that?"** – Hopefully, when you read the first phrase you'll see it's redundant. *Repeat* means to do or say it *again,* so using both words in this phrase comes under the Department of Redundancy Department... meaning it's redundant.

3. Yourself and myself vs. **You and me** – 99% of the time people use *yourself* and/or *myself* when they should just use *you* and/or *me.* For instance, when someone says, "Folks like *yourself* and *myself* don't need no grammar book," what they should say is, "Folks like *you* and *me* don't need no grammar book after this one." Even when referring to just one person, it should be "Folks like *you*" or "Folks like *me*" and not *yourself* and *myself.*

4. Affidavid vs. **Affidavit** – A written statement made under oath is an *affidavit.* There's no such thing as an affidavid. *Affidavit* is one of those Latin words that influences so much of our language; it translates as "a written statement or pledge confirmed by oath."

5. Heighth vs. **Height:** Although length, breadth, width, and depth are all words, heighth is not. It's *height.* Some dictionaries may be starting to include it, but mainly to point out that it's a mistake.

Don't Use Undefined Pronouns!

Listening to someone using undefined pronouns is frustrating. You're left wondering what *it* is or who *they* are. But fixing it is easier than you think! First, let's define an undefined pronoun.

An *undefined pronoun* is one that's used when the noun it's replacing hasn't been specified yet.

Reminder: pronouns are simply words that replace a noun in a sentence. They're used to avoid repeating the same nouns over and over again. But for them to be understood, the noun they're replacing must first be specified.

> **Example 1 – with only undefined pronouns:** *"He* took *it* for a walk. At times *he* used a leash, but *he* also had a carriage. Most people looked at *him* as if *he* were crazy, but not *her."*

In this example we're left with several questions: Who is *he*? What is *it*? Who is *she*?" None of these pronouns had been defined before they were used.

> **Example 2 – without pronouns:** *"Billy* took *his cat* for a walk. At times *Billy* used a leash, but *Billy* also had a carriage. Most people looked at *Billy* as if *he* were crazy, but not *Sarah."*

Repeating the word *Billy* sounds awkward – that's why we use pronouns. We don't want Billy to sound awkward!

> **Example 3 – with pronouns, after *he* is defined:** *Billy* took *his cat* for a walk. At times *he* used a leash, but *he* also had a carriage. Most people looked at *him* as if *he* were crazy, but not *Sarah."* (She was a crazy cat person herself, and she was glad we finally defined the pronoun because she was dying to know his name.)

In example 3, once the noun, *Billy*, is specified, the pronouns make total sense... and to Sarah a catwalk makes total sense... after all, she was a model. ;-)

Here's another example where *undefined pronouns* raise several questions:

Example 1: "She went out of her way to get it for him."

Who is *she*? What is *it* that she went out of her way to get? And who is *he (him)*? *She*, *it*, and *him* are all *undefined pronouns*. They should represent nouns that were previously mentioned, but in this example those haven't been specified yet.

Here's how the sentence *could* have been stated, without using undefined pronouns:

Example 2: "Susan when out of her way to get a live lobster for Dave." (Actually, she got me two... and two more for herself!)

If the nouns were specified in advance, as should have happened, the sentence in example 1 would then be totally valid as stated:

Example 3: "Dave had been craving a live lobster ever since he saw the ad for Larry's Lobster Pound on TV. Susan went shopping, and at the third store she finally found some. *She went out of her way to get it for him.*"

When I hear someone using undefined pronouns, I usually ask for clarification. They may think I'm being an asshole and just giving them a hard time, which may be true, but if you want people to really listen, then it's up to *you* to be clear in what you're saying. It's the speaker's responsibility to communicate clearly so the listener isn't left wondering and doesn't have to make assumptions.

My recommendation to people who do this a lot (not *alot*) is to simply slow down. Whether it's about undefined pronouns or anything else in this book, slowing down and speaking more deliberately lets your brain catch up to your mouth, and the right words are more often likely to emerge. And sometimes no words come out, which is often for the best! (Trust me on this one.)

Summary

First, thank you for reading this book. If you got this far, you deserve a medal (or is it metal?), especially for putting up with my off-beat humor, my political and bodily function digressions, and my sometimes-snooty attitude. And thank you for putting up with my multiple shameless plugs to buy the book, too.

I hope you found a few things in this book that will help you *Smarten the F*ck Up*. Grammar rules can be very intimidating and confusing, so I've tried to present the content in simple language while focusing on the 99% of common mistakes most of us – including me (not *myself*) – make. It's the 1% that twists peoples' brains into knots and causes them to donate their grammar books to Goodwill. My goal is to never see a copy of *Smarten the F*ck Up* in a Goodwill store!

If someone in your family, group of friends, or co-workers needs to *Smarten the F*ck Up*, please share this book with them. They'll thank you… eventually. It's also a great reference book, so you may want to hang on to your copy and recommend they get their own, or give them one as a present… it makes a great gift!

Smarten the F*ck Up is a great conversation starter on your coffee table, too, or you could keep one in the bathroom for when friends come over (just check for missing pages when they leave). Some have also said it's a handy book to pull out in the middle of a conversation… or not.

My last, but not least, suggestion is that English teachers consider using this book as the basis for a class. Although some examples may be a bit crass, they make the lessons more memorable than your typical grammar book. I think it would help produce a more grammatically correct generation, especially when so many now rely on auto-correct for everything.

On a more serious note, this, from the Introduction, bears repeating in this final chapter:

Whenever you express yourself, follow the advice of Robert Louis Stevenson who said, "Don't write merely to be understood. Write so that you cannot possibly be misunderstood." This advice has been central and essential to a lot of my work over the years. *It applies to speaking, too.* We all want to be understood, so it's up to us to ensure we're critically clear in what we're saying.

Here's one last bit of advice on communicating effectively. While it's not really about grammar, it's valuable advice I received from my wonderful ex-mother-in-law, Grace. For some reason she felt I needed to hear this... and often:

"God gave you two ears and one mouth for a reason. You should listen twice as much as you speak."

Her words usually came while sitting around a campfire drinking a few Manhattans, made by her wonderful husband, Vic. RIP Grace and Vic. You were both amazing people, and this was amazing advice. So amazing that I'm passing it on.

I would add this to Grace's advice: When you listen, ask questions about what you hear. When you show sincere interest, people will remember you for making them feel heard more than for what you said. This especially applies in relationships... and some of us learn this the hard way. ;-)

May this advice, as well as the advice in all the other chapters of this book, help you *Smarten the F*ck Up* and become a smarter – and maybe even better – person.

I wish you the best of luck in your *Smarten the F*ck Up* journey!

About the Author

As a constant student of the English language, I have curiously questioned many words, phrases, metaphors, similes, idioms, etc. to understand their meaning, while finding ways to twist them into something other than what they are to make people laugh. Puns are my specialty… and dad jokes, too. If I had a nickel for every time one of my kids rolled their eyes and said, "Ba-dum ching!" I wouldn't have to sell this book, although I would have probably still written it.

As a writer, I've created everything from blog posts, websites, brochures, and marketing copy to poetry and songs. I've also edited the work of other authors and provided publishing services. I thoroughly enjoy playing with words and sharpening my wit around a campfire with close friends and a few beers. I've also spent considerable time scowling at those who make social media posts with many of the common mistakes presented in this book. Now that you've read it, if we ever become friends, I won't have to scowl at you!

Made in the USA
Las Vegas, NV
30 November 2022

60788815R00120